S0-BDP-117

Stockholm

Berlitz Publishing Company, Inc.
Princeton   Mexico City   London   Eschborn   Singapore

Berlitz Trademark Reg. U.S. Patent Office and other countries
Marca Registrada

Text:	Norman Renouf
Editor:	Media Content Marketing, Inc.
Photography:	Courtesy of the Danish and Swedish Tourist Boards except pages 25, 31, 32, 33, 39, 43, 44, 92 Jon Davison and pages 5, 14, 67 Bobby Andstrom
Cover Photo:	Courtesy of the Danish and Swedish Tourist Boards
Photo Editor:	Naomi Zinn
Layout:	Media Content Marketing, Inc.
Cartography:	Raffaele De Gennaro

Although the publisher tries to insure the accuracy of all the information in this book, changes are inevitable and errors may result. The publisher cannot be responsible for any resulting loss, inconvenience, or injury. If you find an error in this guide, please let the editors know by writing to Berlitz Publishing Company, 400 Alexander Park, Princeton, NJ 08540-6306.

ISBN 2-8315-7754-3

Printed in Italy
010/104 REV

CONTENTS

• A (☞) in the text denotes a highly recommended sight

Stockholm

THE CITY AND ITS PEOPLE

Stockholm, the capital of Sweden, is well deserving of the honor of being considered one of the world's most beautiful cities. Dramatically situated at a point where the Baltic Sea and the waters of Lake Mälaren collide and fight for supremacy, the city has been splendidly endowed by nature. In fact, only the city center to the north is situated on the mainland, with the rest being spread unevenly, although gracefully, over 14 islands that are connected by no fewer than 40 bridges. This impressive scenario inspired the Swedish novelist Selma Lagerlöf to cleverly describe Stockholm as "the city that floats on water." Natural beauty, though, is just a part of its charm. Stockholm also has a glittering array of monuments, museums, buildings, restaurants, and other fascinating attractions that will keep visitors thoroughly absorbed throughout their stay, whatever its length.

Founded by Birger Jarl (Jarl means earl) in the middle of the 13th century, Stockholm doubled in size during the 15th century. In 1523 it was captured by Gustav Vasa after he finally vanquished the Danes. Finding the city in a state of great disrepair, he started many construction projects including the Tre Konor castle. However, Gustav Vasa's son, King Johan III, transformed the castle into a Renaissance palace, making a grand impression on the city. Stockholm had to wait until 1634 before becoming Sweden's capital, then with a population of just 15,000. Between 1635 and 1685, the population grew dramatically to 60,000 — the largest relative increase ever in the city. In 1671 a German, Nicodemus Tessin the Elder, became the city's first appointed city architect, and he and a Frenchman, Simon de

The golden sunshine sparkles on Riddarholmen on a beautiful winter's day.

la Vallée (and later their sons), were responsible for changing Stockholm's architectural style. Among their many new projects were the new royal palace, the classical royal palace of Drottningholm, and the very beautiful Riddarhuset (House of Nobility). A dramatic fire in 1697 caused much damage, and in 1709, the major defeat by the Russians under Peter the Great at the battle of Poltava brought about the end of Sweden's status as a major power. The peace treaty subsequently signed with Russia was so unfavorable that it left Sweden, and thus Stockholm, severely financially handicapped. Major building works such as the royal palace were suspended. By this time the city's population had decreased to just 45,000, the same level as fifty years earlier. King Karl (Charles) XII's murder in 1718 brought about the end of absolute monarchy, and heralded the Frihetstiden (Age of Liberty in Sweden). Parliament passed a new tax law in 1727, thus enabling work on the palace to begin again. In the next year, Tessin the Younger died and was succeeded as the director of public works by his son, Carl Gustaf, who became formally responsible for work on the palace.

The Age of Liberty brought an increase in trade and manufacturing to the city, which allowed the population to recover to 75,000 by 1780. The death of King Gustav III, in 1792, ushered in a period of political instability and subsequent economic decline, which was compounded in 1809 when Finland was lost to Russia. Stockholm, for the first time in nearly 600 years, was no longer the geographic center of the kingdom.

The first half of the new century brought more architectural changes in Stockholm — the only major building projects were military ones. The population fell and rose during this period, falling to around 65,000 in 1810 and yet reaching 100,000 by 1856. The Western Sweden main railroad was opened in 1862, and the Northern Sweden main line was completed in 1866. Work began that year to link the two, with the connection running over the island of Riddarholmen completed in 1871 and coinciding with the opening of the neo-Renaissance style Centralstationen (Central Station), then the second largest building in Stockholm after the Royal Palace.

These days, the city is not only the seat of the national parliament, the royal palace, and many other places of historical interest, but also is the country's financial and business center. In recent decades, an ambitious building program has added a whole new aspect to the city. In the center, classic buildings have given way to more modern, plainer ones, and offices have replaced apartments, forcing many former residents out to the mushrooming suburbs. Even though Sweden is a large country — the fifth largest in Europe after Russia, Ukraine, Spain, and France — more than 1.5 million people, over one-sixth of the total population, crowds into the Stockholm area.

Stockholm has an area of 4,900 sq km (1,892 sq miles) and, although 30% of this is water, another 30% is made up of "green zones." The different islands and districts that make up Stockholm are often so unlike one another that they create the illusion of a series of miniature and only distantly-related cities. Each has its own distinct charm and mood.

Take Gamla Stan, the Old Town, for instance. It was in this island of antiquity in the heart of the city, around 1252, that Stockholm was born. A stroll along its many cobbled alleys and twisting lanes, flanked by perfectly preserved 15th- and 16th-century houses, some with copper roofs, takes you back to medieval times. By way of contrast, Norrmalm, the northern sector of town and location of Sergels Torg, represents the world of the late 20th century: It boasts glass skyscrapers, shopping malls, underpasses, overpasses, and the traffic circles of the city center. Adjoining Norrmalm, to the east, is Östermalm, a highly fashionable neighborhood of stately apartment buildings, where many of the city's foreign embassies are located. Kungsholmen, the island just west of the city center, hosts the municipal administration and is graced by the strikingly handsome Stadshuset (City Hall) rising gracefully from the shore of Lake Mälaren. To experience another face of Stockholm visit Södermalm, the huge, hilly southern island overlooking the rest of the city. Its lofty location and numerous artists' studios give Södermalm a kind of Montmartre atmosphere. Here you'll find charming clusters of old wooden cottages in rural settings.

Cultural life in Stockholm thrives today as never before, especially the performing arts, which receive large government subsidies. Public money supports the 200-year-old Royal Opera, one of the best in the world, as well as the excellent Royal Dramatic Theatre. The city also boasts over 70 museums. At one time nightlife was almost non-existent in Stockholm, but along with the new architecture has come a virtual explosion of nightclubs, pubs, and discotheques; the city now swings after dark. Eating habits have also changed, with foreign cuisine — Chinese, French, Italian, and many others — supplementing, if not quite replacing, traditional Swedish food in many restaurants.

A glance at shop windows or people on the street confirms that this is quite an affluent city. Stockholmers live and dress well, and in the stores you'll find the best of Sweden's famous design products, including superb crystal from the glassworks district of Småland in the southeast part of the country.

What about the Swedes themselves? One could generalize by saying that they are a very pragmatic, orderly, and reserved peo-

Stroll along the black-and-white tiles of the underground in Stockholm, the world's longest art gallery.

A day of shopping at Nybrogatan is a day well spent in Stockholm.

ple with a strong sense of social consciousness. They have created many innovative, humane laws that have become models for the world. The Swedes remain close to nature. Come summer the family retreats to its modest stuga, or cottage, amid rustic woodland for a taste of the simpler life. From the months of July to September, armies of berry-pickers and mushroom-hunters invade the forests.

As a summer city, Stockholm — and especially its lovely environs — is hard to beat. There is music and dancing in the city parks, concerts at the Royal Palace, recitals in many of the museums and churches. And, at this time, the city's graceful silhouette is bathed in the eerily beautiful midsummer light. Stockholm is well worth visiting at other times of the year as well. There are some who admire it most in its autumn glory, or when the buds open in the spring. And few would deny the enchanting beauty of the city in the dead of winter, when snow makes picture-postcard scenery out of narrow lanes and tiny squares; and the bays, channels, and canals freeze over, allowing Stockholmers to walk and ski over the waterways and inlets of the sea. It is fair to say that the spectacular seasonal transformations belong to the experience of Stockholm just as truly as its architectural juncture of old and new.

A BRIEF HISTORY

Archaeologists have established that Swedish history began somewhere around 12,000 B.C., when the miles-thick blanket of ice covering the whole continent began to melt. In the subsequent millennia, nomadic tribes of hunters and fishermen followed the receding ice cap northwards to the area that is now Sweden. In about 3000 B.C. the inhabitants of the area were cultivating the land, raising livestock, and living together in communities. Magnificent Bronze Age artifacts, including weapons and ornaments, indicate an early period of prosperity. Mysterious rock carvings of animals and people also survive from the prehistoric period.

By the time that Swedes are mentioned for the first instance in recorded history, however, conditions had altered substantially. This was in A.D. 98, in Germania, where Roman historian Tacitus described the Sviones, or Svear tribe, as fierce warriors with mighty fleets of ships. They were based around Lake Mälaren, gradually rose to a position of dominance over neighboring tribes, and by their seafaring exploits heralded the beginning of the Viking Age (A.D. 800–1050).

The Vikings

The Vikings are best remembered for their ferocious raids on countries that were richer than they. They simply helped themselves to what they wanted, rather than eke out an existence in their harsh homeland. Some of the battles and exploits of this time are recorded on the thousands of rune stones to be found in Sweden.

However, the popular image of Vikings as the villains in history has been undergoing revision. Modern scholarship has revealed that the Vikings were also remarkable poets and artists,

Vikings were busy in Sweden — there's proof in this heavily decorated rune stone.

explorers and settlers, who made many positive contributions to the territories they occupied. In their famous long ships, manned by as many as 50 oarsmen, these extraordinary seamen pushed west to England, Ireland, and Scotland, then overran large areas of France, established new colonies in the Faroes, Iceland, and Greenland, and finally reached the shores of North America. And those Swedish Vikings who turned towards the east travelled along the rivers of Russia, establishing control over Novgorod and Kiev, and went on as far as Constantinople.

The Vikings' admirable navigational skills also equipped them for far-flung trading expeditions, and they soon became merchants as well as marauders. These heathens cannily turned to religion to improve their commercial dealings with Christian countries.

Early Christianity

Throughout the Viking period, Christian missionaries, mostly English and German monks, were active in Sweden. The first Christian church was founded in about A.D. 830 in Birka by Ansgar, a monk from Picardy.

Christianizing Sweden was an uphill battle, to say the least, and there were sporadic lapses into paganism as late as the 12th century. In Uppsala, for instance, yearly sacrificial feasts were held in honor of the Norse gods. By the 13th century, however, the Church had become a dominant force in the country. The first archbishop, with a diocese in Uppsala, was appointed in 1164, and many churches were built during this period.

During the 13th century, a time of strife and contending factions, one important figure to emerge was Birger Jarl. Brother-in-law to the king, Jarl promoted the idea of a strong central government and also encouraged trade with other nations. When the king died, Birger Jarl had his own son elected heir to the throne. He is also credited with founding Stockholm, in about 1252, as a fort to protect against pirates.

The outstanding personality of the following century was St. Birgitta, a religious mystic. Born in 1303, this remarkable woman was a prominent court figure, wife of a nobleman, and mother of eight children. She founded a monastic order and church in the town of Vadstena in central Sweden, and her book, *Revelations* — translated into Latin and widely read in the Christian world — is considered a masterpiece of medieval literature. St. Birgitta died in Rome, but her remains were brought back to Vadstena and buried in the church there.

The Kalmar Union

The so-called Kalmar Union was formed in 1397 to counteract the rapidly increasing power of the German Hanseatic League of the time. It united Sweden, Denmark, and Norway under a single ruler, the very able Queen Margareta of Denmark, making it Europe's largest kingdom.

The Swedes came to resent the dominance of the Danes and many were opposed to the union. In the 1430s they were led in a popular rebellion by the great Swedish hero Engelbrekt, who also assembled the first Swedish parliament in 1435. This Riksdag, which included representatives of the four estates — nobles, clergy, burghers, and peasants — elected Engelbrekt regent of Sweden. Soon afterward he was murdered and the unpopular union limped along until 1520. In that year the Scandinavian monarch, Christian II of Denmark, ruthlessly executed scores of Swedish noblemen, opponents who had been accused of heresy. However, instead of eliminating revolt, the "Stockholm Blood Bath" unleashed a popular reaction that led to the disintegration of the despised Kalmar Union.

One of the noblemen who escaped death, Gustav Vasa, called on the peasants of the province of Dalarna to rebel against the Danish tyrant. With a ragtag army supported by foreign mercenaries, he succeeded in routing the Danes. He was crowned king in 1523 at the age of 27, and his dynamic reign dominated the 16th century.

History in the Field

Sweden's elongated landscape — stretching about a thousand miles from north to south — can be compared to a vast open-air museum with fascinating artifacts from the dim past.

Foremost are the Viking rune stones scattered throughout the country. These strange memorials record history and perpetuate myths. The hieroglyphics inscribed on their surfaces recount the everyday and heroic moments of the Viking warriors for whom the rune stones were raised. A fine selection is displayed in the Historiska Museet in Stockholm (see page 57). Other features of the landscape dating from far-off times include cromlechs (stone burial enclosures), fabulous rock carvings of boats, animals, and people, and Viking burial mounds.

Best of all, perhaps, are Sweden's lovely medieval country churches. Filled with remarkably well-preserved naïve wood sculptures, stained-glass windows, altar paintings, and murals, they form an integral part of the countryside.

Gustav Vasa was a strong-willed leader who reshaped the nation, earning himself the sobriquet "Father of His Country." He reorganized the state administration and stabilized its finances by, among other methods, confiscating all of the church's considerable property holdings. After he died in 1560, three of his sons ruled Sweden in turn, and the Vasa dynasty survived for almost 150 years.

Sweden as a World Power

Foremost among the Vasa kings was Gustavus Adolphus, crowned Gustav II Adolf in 1611 at the age of 17. He promoted trade and industry and extended the borders of Sweden by conquests in Russia and Poland. Under his leadership Sweden became, for a time, the greatest power in 17th-century Europe. A few years later, in 1632, Gustav II Adolf was killed in a battle at Lutzen defending the Protestant cause in the Thirty Years' War in Germany.

As his daughter Kristina was only six when Gustavus Adolphus died, the extremely capable Count Axel Oxenstierna served as regent. Kristina was crowned in 1644. A very gifted but eccentric woman, she hated women and only socialized with men. Although making her court a brilliant salon, inviting to her capital famous European intellectuals such as the French philosopher Descartes, she was known to swear like a sailor. Ten years later, however, the queen startled the nation by abdicating; she converted to Catholicism and settled in Rome. She died in 1689 and is buried in St. Peter's Cathedral there.

During the 17th century, Sweden, which had previously annexed Estonia, gained additional ground in the Baltic and along the German coasts and extended its borders into parts of Denmark and Norway. Sweden also established its first colony in America, in what is now Delaware, which was later captured by Britain. Sweden's final moments as a great power occurred under Karl (Charles) XII, who became monarch of the realm in 1697 at the age of 15. He is one of the most celebrated and controversial figures in the history of Sweden. Encouraged by a series of brilliant victories on the battlefield, the young king led his army deep into the interior of Russia in 1708–1709, where he met with a disastrous defeat at Poltava in the Ukraine in the latter year.

After an extended exile in Turkey, Karl XII took up arms once more and was killed in Norway in 1718. His death marked the end of Sweden's Baltic Empire. Only Finland and part of Pomerania remained, and decades of unremitting warfare had left the country weak and in debt.

The Golden Age

The years of peace that followed were a golden age of culture and science in Sweden. During this period, Carolus Linnaeus laid the foundations for modern botanical science by classifying the flora of the world, and Anders Celsius, the physicist and astronomer, developed the centigrade thermometer using a scale of 100 degrees between the freezing and boiling points of water.

Culture flourished during the reign of Gustav III (1771–1792). The king, an ardent supporter of music, literature, and art, founded the Royal Opera and the Swedish Academy (the Academy awards the Nobel Prize for Literature) to counter French influence and encourage the Swedish language. He also gave the nation what is known as the elegant "Gustavian" style, the local version of Louis XVI style.

However, Gustav III was mortally wounded in an assassination attempt at a masked ball in the Stockholm Opera House, and Sweden was subsequently drawn into the Napoleonic Wars. In 1809 Finland, after having been a part of Sweden for 600 years, was possessed by Russia under an

A 15th-century sculpture of St. George and the Dragon ornaments the Stockholm church of Storkyrkan.

agreement between Czar Alexander I and Napoleon. In 1818 the Bernadotte dynasty was "imported" from France and a field marshal under Napoleon, Jean Baptiste Bernadotte, was elected to the Swedish throne (as Karl XIV Johan), in the hope of obtaining French assistance in recovering Finland. In the event, Sweden participated in a final offensive to defeat Napoleon, with whom Denmark was allied. One of the results was Denmark's 1814 cession of Norway, which remained attached to Sweden until 1905.

An agricultural crisis hit Sweden towards the end of the 19th century. The hard times caused hundreds of thousands of Swedes to emigrate to America in the 1880s.

The 20th Century

The 20th century saw Sweden shifting rapidly from a farming economy to an industrial one. More and more people moved from rural areas to towns and cities. The emigration to America also continued, so that by 1930 about a million Swedes, one out of five, had settled in the New World.

At the same time, the power of the labor unions and their ally, the Social Democratic Party, founded in 1889, was increasing. Hjalmar Branting, the great socialist leader, became Prime Minister in 1920, setting the stage for vast social reforms that were to make Sweden the world's leading welfare state. Swedes may pay one of the highest rates of tax in the world to support cradle-to-grave security, but most of them feel that they get a lot in return for their money. This includes housing subsidies, maternity leave, child allowances, free hospital care, old-age pensions, and a host of other benefits — not to mention the right to five weeks paid vacation annually. These and other social measures in operation, however, fall far short of classic socialism, and the bulk of Swedish industry is still controlled by private interests. The solid success of Swedish industry having exploited effectively the few natural resources — namely iron ore and timber — has not only made the welfare state possible, but has also allowed for one of the world's highest standards of living.

Swedish technical genius has played a significant role in building an affluent society as well. Many of Sweden's international companies have been developed on the basis of Swedish inventions such as dynamite (invented by Alfred Nobel; see page 21), the modern calculator (Odhner), and the important three-phase alternating electrical current system (Jonas Wenström).

Sweden remains a constitutional monarchy with the king as head of state, but actual power rests solely with parliament, which since 1971 has consisted of a single chamber with 350 members. The Social Democrats — who held office for a record 44 years before losing power to a coalition of non-socialist parties between 1976 and 1982 — have been the dominant faction in 20th-century Swedish politics. Nonetheless, the country has mostly been governed by con-

The Pacifist Who Invented Dynamite

Alfred Nobel (1833–1896), became a first-rate chemist while still in his teens. Inventor, engineer, and industrialist, he held a total of 355 patents during his lifetime.

Highly paradoxical is that Nobel, a pacifist at heart, invented dynamite, which proved such a boon to modern warfare. He also patented blasting gelatin, a substance more powerful than dynamite, and invented smokeless gunpowder. These products formed the basis of his industrial empire, which spread across five continents.

Alfred Nobel established the celebrated Nobel prizes in his will, drawn up a year before his death. These were for physics and chemistry, to be awarded by the Swedish Academy of Sciences; for physiological or medical works, to be awarded by the Karolinska Institute in Stockholm; for literature, to be awarded by the Academy in Stockholm; and for champions of peace, to be awarded by a committee of five persons to be elected by the Norwegian Storting. They were to go to those who "shall have conferred the greatest benefit on mankind" with the stipulation that "no consideration whatever shall be given to the nationality of the candidates." His entire fortune, which amounted to many millions of dollars, was dedicated to this purpose.

First awarded in 1901, the Nobel prizes for the first four categories have been given at the glittering Nobel Dinner held at the Stadshuset (City Hall) of Stockholm on 10 December every year. Nobel directed that the Peace prize be awarded in Oslo, which at his death, and until 1905, was part of Sweden. Since then this prize has ironically been awarded in the capital of a foreign country.

Although Sweden is a very modern nation, remnants of the past, like this 16th-century castle, are around every bend.

sensus, with political decisions reached by discreet compromise. All of the nation's political parties have supported the broad outlines of the welfare state.

The 20th century has been a time of almost uninterrupted stability and peace for Sweden. It fought its last war in 1814, and adopted a strict policy of neutrality that kept it out of both world wars.

Notwithstanding their capacity for neutrality and compromise, Swedes make a concerted effort to avoid isolationist policies. The country has supported the United Nations since its inception and, after voting in a 1994 referendum to join the European Union, it became a member the following year. As a reflection of its now-European status, Stockholm was selected as the 1998 Cultural Capital of Europe.

WHERE TO GO

At first glance, visitors to Stockholm may feel that the unusual, if not unique, geographical combination of islands and water might make the city difficult to navigate and somewhat confusing. However, this is most certainly not the case. In fact, most people will find themselves in Norrmalm, the more modern city center, where a combination of proximity and an array of efficient public transportation — buses, subway, tramcars and ferry boats — makes getting around easier than one might think.

Visitors will find it extremely helpful to acclimate themselves to Stockholm by taking a boat tour of the city. Stockholm Sightseeing, Tel. (08) 587 140 20; web site <www.stockholmsightseeing.com>, offers several trips. A good suggestion is to take the 2-hour *Under the Bridges of Stockholm* tour. This takes in both the Baltic Sea and Lake Mälaren sides of Stockholm and offers an extremely informative multilingual commentary. A ticket costs 140kr, and tours depart on the hour from Strömkajen, just in front of the Grand Hôtel.

A bus tour is also helpful, and City Sightseeing, Tel. (08) 587 140 44; web site <www.citysightseeing.com>, offers a variety of tours, one of which is the *Stockholm Panorama*. It lasts 1¹/₂ hours and has a multilingual commentary, probably making it the most helpful. It departs from Gustav II Adolfs Torg, in front of the Royal Opera House, almost every hour in the summer.

On these trips you cannot help but notice the huge TV tower, and if you want to get a bird's-eye view of Stockholm and its immediate environs, then this is the place to head for. A Number 69 bus, from Sweden House (the tourist office), will get you there. And the stunning views from the observation platform at the top of the 170 m (511 ft) tall **Kaknästornet**, Tel. (08) 789 24 35, the tallest building in Scandinavia, provide a perfect visual introduction to Stockholm. It is open daily, May–August, 9am–10pm and 10am–9pm in the remaining months. Entrance is 25kr and is included with the Stockholm Card.

Having seen and learned much, you will now be aware that this is a place ideal for wandering around on foot. This is the best way to experience Stockholm's multiple, and more subtle, charms and moods.

CITY CENTER

You will, undoubtedly, be spending a good deal of time in the New Stockholm, or *Norrmalm*, the city's northern sector. This is where the business, banking, shopping, and entertainment facilities are concentrated, as well as the majority of hotels and the railway and bus stations.

Central Stockholm has been almost entirely rebuilt, and you will see a bewildering array of shapes and materials employed to construct the soaring towers of the new buildings. Old streets have been replaced by modern shopping malls with restaurants, cinemas, and boutiques. Nowhere is this more obvious than in **Sergels Torg** (Sergel Square), the focal point of the new city center. Named after the 18th-century court sculptor, Johan Tobias Sergel, it is easily recognized by two unmistakable landmarks, a gigantic glass obelisk rising from a fountain right in the middle of a very busy traffic circle, and the great glass-fronted **Kulturhuset** (House of Culture), which attracts thousands of visitors daily. They come to see films and videos; to peruse art and handicrafts exhibitions; to listen to music, poetry, dramatic readings, and debates, and to visit the cyber-café. Also here is the Stockholm Stadsteatern

Modern sculpture and modern architecture make Sergels Torg — the center of the new city — especially distinct.

(Municipal Theatre), which stages both modern and classical plays in Swedish. In Kulturhuset's innovative library you can sink down in an easy chair fitted out with earphones and listen to an extensive selection of classical, pop, or jazz music on records and tapes. The square's open-air lower level, visible from above and surrounded by a shopping center, is a vast open space and has become a social gathering place.

A short walk through the shopping center, a combination of malls and shopping streets usually animated by the music of street performers, will take you to **Hötorget** (Haymarket Square), the northern end of the row of glass skyscrapers that starts at Sergels Torg. Hötorget's open-air market — selling fresh fruit, vegetables, and flowers six days a week and operating as a flea market on Sunday — adds a touch of color to the square. Also on Hötorget, you will find **Konserthuset** (Concert Hall), a Neo-Classical building distinguished by an unusual façade of Corinthian pillars and bronze portals. The Stockholm Philharmonic Orchestra performs here, but you can hear other kinds of music, from chamber music to pop melodies. In front of the building you will see Carl Milles' **Orpheus Fountain**, one of the late Swedish sculptor's finest works (see page 50).

Double back to Sergels Torg, turn left, and you're on **Hamngatan**, one of the main shopping streets. Its tenants include NK (short for Nordiska Kompaniet), Sweden's

The young-at-heart will have great fun ice-skating in the city center in Kungsträgården.

biggest department store, alongside newcomers like Gallerian, a mall with many stores and restaurants. At Hamngatan 27, **Sverigehuset** (Sweden House) supplies information about Sweden. Inside, a regional tourist office provides maps and guides of Stockholm and surrounding areas, as well as a money exchange office, souvenir shop, and bookshop. Tickets for the theater, concerts, and sports events can also be purchased here.

Next door is Stockholm's liveliest park, **Kungsträdgården** (Royal Gardens), stretching from Hamngatan down to the waters of Strömmen. Established as a royal pleasure garden in the 16th century for the exclusive use of the Swedish aristocracy and the court, Kungsträdgården has now become a favorite gathering place for locals and visitors during the summer months. Encircled by cafés and restaurants you will find a long, rectangular pond with fountains; an outdoor stage for rock, chamber music, and choral concerts; botanical exhibits; and statues.

Continuing east on Hamngatan, you will pass the **Hallwylska** (see Highlights, page 78). This patrician mansion, completed in 1898, was built for Walter and Wilelmina von Hallwyl. He came from one of Europe's oldest noble families and she was the daughter of a prosperous steel and wood magnate. She was responsible for the amazing collections that can be seen today in the 70 perfectly preserved rooms, filled to overflowing with Gobelin tapestries, china figurines, Flemish and Dutch paintings, antique furniture, and assorted objets d'art. The mansion was surprisingly modern, with electricity, central heating, running hot and cold water, a bath and shower, and even indoor wood-panelled toilets. The Hallwyls donated the house to the state in 1920 and, after Walter's death in 1921, Wilhelmina left complex instructions in her will (including the exact length — to

Sweden's national theater, the Kunglia Dramatiska Teatern, is located at Nybroviken.

the minute — of tours), as to how the museum was to be run after her death. She died in 1930 and, in fact, nothing has changed in the mansion since the day the family lived here.

Farther on, at Nybroplan, you will find the attractive façade of the **Kungliga Dramatiska Teatern** (Royal Dramatic Theatre), where such notable performers as Greta Garbo, Ingrid Bergman, and Max von Sydow began their careers. Before his death in 1953, American playwright Eugene O'Neill bequeathed his last plays to the Dramatic Theatre, and their world premières (including that of *Long Day's Journey into Night*) were staged here.

From Nybroplan, cross between the water and the rather pleasant Berzeli Park, dominated by Berns restaurant and bar, and walk along Nybrokajen, a quayside street lined with boats. As you turn the corner at the bottom the island, Skeppsholmen will be across a narrow stretch of water, and can be reached by way of a small bridge, Skeppsholmsbron. Crossing it will bring you to two museums really worth investigation, **Östasiatiska Museet** (Museum of Far Eastern Antiquities) and the **Moderna Museet** (Museum of Modern Art).

Crossing back over the bridge you will be immediately welcomed by the imposing façade of the **Nationalmuseum** (National Museum). Leave there, and continue along Södra Blasieholmshamnen, where you will pass the impressive Grand Hôtel to the right. It overlooks the tourist boats run by Stockholm Sightseeing on your left. Immediately facing you, and at the foot of the Kungsträdgården, is the small, but nevertheless charming, Karl XII's Torg. It is dominated by a statue of the man himself, King Charles XII, Sweden's most celebrated historical figure. Behind this park the outline of the 17th-century church **Jakobs Kyrka** dominates. It is worth a moment here to look at the marvelous portals, particularly the one on the southern side, which dates from 1644.

Just ahead is Gustav Adolfs Torg, a large square with an equestrian statue of King Gustavus Adolphus, the Swedish hero of the Thirty Years' War. On the east side of the square you will see **Operan** (Royal Opera), housed in a sombre Baroque-style building from 1898. King Gustav III, a great patron of the arts, founded the opera in 1773. It was here (in the original opera house) that he was shot and killed some twenty years later at a masked ball. Incidentally, Verdi used this drama as the basis for his opera *The Masked Ball*. Swedes are proud of the Royal Opera's long and distinguished history. Some of the world's greatest singers got their start here, from Jenny Lind, the 19th-century "Swedish Nightingale" who made a fabulously successful tour around the United States, to Jussi Björling and Birgit Nilsson. This remarkable institution has a breathtaking output of nearly 400 performances of opera and ballet each season.

☛ GAMLA STAN

The high island rising between the waters of the Baltic Sea and Lake Mälaren is now known as **Gamla Stan** — the Old Town. However, in the 13th century it was called Stadsholmen and its naturally defensive position (between two narrow channels of water connecting the sea and lake), made it an ideal location for Birger Jarl to construct a fortress and begin the foundations of the city. Consequently, Stockholm's history is concentrated in Gamla Stan and its cobbled lanes and winding alleys house mansions, palaces, and soaring spires steeped in history. Just walking around, you will get the impression of being transported back centuries in time.

Exploring Gamla Stan is a must for every visitor to Stockholm. Starting from Gustav Adolfs Torg cross over the gracefully arched bridge of Norrbro. The massive façade of the Royal Palace beckons, but before going there spend a few mo-

The picture of tranquility, Gamla Stan is surrounded by the waters of the Baltic Sea and Lake Mälaren.

The Swedish parliament makes many important decisions right here in the heart of the Old Town.

ments on the first little island — one of the four comprising Gamla Stan. On your right will be the **Riksdagshuset** (House of Parliament), Tel. (08) 786 40 00, with free guided tours June–August Monday–Friday 12:30pm and 2pm and on Saturday and Sunday at 1pm. To the left, steps lead down to a charming park, **Stromparterren** and, although it is home to the Museum of Medieval Stockholm, a short stop at the café along the banks of the Norrström channel shouldn't be missed. This is where the roiling waters of the Baltic and Lake Mälaren meet and fight each other for supremacy. You will probably see fishermen that partake of their hobby either from the bankside or standing in the water. The Stockholm authorities actually encourage this. No permit is required, and there is even a weighing scale in the corner of the park to check if a trophy fish has been caught.

No small undertaking — the Royal Palace is one of the most enormous houses in the world!

Now cross the next bridge over the narrow Stallkanalen waterway, and head up the hill to the **Kungliga Slottet** (Royal Palace; see Highlights page 78). Built on the site of the original Tre Kronor (Three Crowns) castle, it was commissioned by King Karl XI, and the architect Nicodemus Tessin the Younger began work on it in 1692. However, a combination of a fire in 1697 and a subsequent poor economy delayed continuation until 1728. It wasn't until 1754 that King Adolf Fredrik was able to move in, ending the royal family's 57 years of residence in the Wrangelska palace on the island of Riddarholmen. It is still the official residence of His Majesty the King, and until the present monarch, Carl XVI Gustaf, decided to reside at Drottningholm, it was known as one of the biggest palaces in the world (over 600 rooms) still to be inhabited by royalty.

Kungliga Slottet is remarkably accessible to the public, although parts, or all, may be closed for affairs of state. Anyone can walk through the inner courtyard, and the main parts of the building are open to visitors. Be sure not to miss the beautifully preserved Rococo interior of the **Royal Chapel**, and Queen Kristina's silver throne in the Hall of State. Among other palace highlights are the **royal apartments** and **galleries** with magnificent Baroque interiors, containing priceless 17th-century Gobelin tapestries, paintings, china, jewelry, and furniture collected over the centuries by kings and queens. The royal jewels are displayed in the **treasury** (Skattkammaren) and include the king's crown, first used for Erik XIV's coronation in 1561, and the queen's crown, designed in 1751 for Queen Lovisa Ulrika, which is spectacularly studded with almost 700 diamonds. In addition to housing the Treasury, the **Palace Museum**

in the cellar has artifacts from the Middle Ages, and the Museum of Antiquities exhibits Classical sculpture brought from Italy by King Gustav III during the 1780s.

Also located in the complex is **Livrustkammaren** (Royal Armory; see Stockholm Highlights page 78). Formerly housed in the Nordic Museum, Livrustkammaren is a fascinating collection of the weapons and

The helmets of the royal guards may be more dangerous than their guns.

costumes of Swedish kings. Some of the more esoteric exhibits you'll see include a horse ridden by Gustavus Adolphus when he fell in the Battle of Lützen in 1632, cleverly preserved by a taxidermist; the uniform that Charles XII was wearing when he was fatally wounded in the trenches while besieging Fredrikshald, Norway, in 1718; and the costume Gustav III wore when he was murdered at the Opera Ball, together with the assassin's gun and mask.

No visit to the Kungliga Slottet is complete without taking time to witness the ritual **changing of the guard** in the outer courtyard (see Highlights, page 78). Immensely popular, it is estimated that over 400,000 spectators view it annually. The approximately 14,000 conscripts who serve as guards each year, 9,000 here and the rest at Drottningholm, come from about 50 military units and schools from all over Sweden. And this is just not an honorary force, but also an important part of military readiness in Stockholm. That said, Sweden, once a mighty military power in northern Europe, has not been involved in a war since the early 19th century. The event is certainly ceremonial, although there is also an element of humor and the formality is slightly less than that found in similar situations elsewhere. In fact, on one occasion, two guards hilariously marched away from the rest of the troop instead of with it!

Two streets emanate southwards from either side of the Kungliga Slottet, Västerlanggatan to the west and Österlänggatan to the east, finally curving together at the small square of Järntorget (the Iron Market Square). These two streets adjoined the original city walls, and the area inside them plus the palace actually constitute the original Old Town.

Just south of the palace on Slottsbacken, and diagonally across from the south façade, is **Storkyrkan** (Great Church),

Tel. (08) 723 30 09. (Open daily, May–August 9am–6pm, until 4pm during winter. Admission free.) It is the city's oldest church, dating from the 13th century, and it has been the coronation site of most of Sweden's kings. Storkyrkan's dull Baroque exterior gives no hint of the beauty of its late-Gothic interior. Of note is the sculptural depiction of St. George and the Dragon, which symbolizes Sweden's struggles to break free of Denmark. The sculpture was executed by Bernt Notke, a wood carver from Lübeck, in the 15th century.

Just a few steps from the church, in **Stortorget** (Great Square), a murderous event known as the "Stockholm Blood Bath" took place in 1520. King Christian II of Denmark ordered some 80 Swedish noblemen beheaded here, and

*There are countless historic places to see
in Stortorget, the oldest city center.*

their heads were piled pyramid-style in the middle of the square. Among the fine old houses on Stortorget is the **Börsen** (Stock Exchange), a handsome building dating from 1776. The Swedish Academy meets here to elect the Nobel Prize winners in literature.

Once you've seen these two principal attractions, the best way to get the feel of the Old Town is to wander around aimlessly. There's something to experience at every turn — antiques shops housed in fine 15th- and 16th-century buildings, former merchant palaces, gabled houses decorated with ornate portals, and charming alleyways with names like **Gåsgränd** (Goose Lane) and **Skeppar Karls Gränd** (Skipper Karl's Lane). You'll also come across art shops, galleries, and smart boutiques selling clothes, handcrafted jewelry, and ceramics. Explore the Old Town without a specific itinerary, but by all means be sure to include some of the spots mentioned below as you meander about.

Västerlånggatan (pedestrian-only), and **Österlånggatan** are interesting and contrasting streets in their own right. The former, lined along its entirety with tourist stores of every description, bars, and restaurants, is much more popular and is usually extremely crowded. At Tyska Brinken make a short detour to the left and go to **Tyska Kyrkan** (German Church). It boasts a fine Baroque exterior and an opulent interior dating from the mid-17th century. Near the end, also on the left, is **Mårten Trotzigs Gränd**, the narrowest street in Stockholm. This steep, lamp-lit, stone stairway is scarcely more than a yard wide and takes you on to Prästgatan. Past **Järntorget,** swing left into Österlånggatan, another long, winding street. Despite being dotted with art galleries, craftsmen's shops, and some fine restaurants, it is noticeably more tranquil. At number 51 is **Den Gyldene Freden** (The Golden Peace), the most famous restaurant in the Old Town.

Its name comes from the Peace of Nystad of 1721, which marked the end of Charles XII's wars. The historic brick cellar rooms are associated with the 18th-century troubadour Carl Michaël Bellman, who dropped by here from time to time. Walking north, you will pass by another statue of St. George and the Dragon and an exquisite restaurant, Pontus in the Greenhouse, at number17, where you can delight in the culinary creations of Pontus Frithiof.

The areas to either side of Österlånggatan and Väster-långgatan are reclaimed land. To the east of the former, narrow picturesque lanes with arched entrances and small streets lead to the long, wide, waterfront thoroughfare of **Skeppsbrokajen**. The structures here are of a grand style, and the quayside is lined with a vast array of vessels. These range from ferry-boats to restaurant boats, a Viking ship for harbor cruises, and the most magnificent cruise ships you are likely to see. The western side of Gamla Stan is somewhat larger, if less attractive, and it is bisected by the rather busy Stora Nygatan. At its northern end is a square called

Finding Your Way

Knowing a few key geographical terms in Swedish may help unravel some of the enigmas of a strange city and help you to find your way around. You should note that the words for "street," "square," and so on are often tacked on to place names, as in Skräddargränd (Tailors' Lane). Here is a list of some of the most common ones you'll come across:

bro	bridge	plan, plats	square
gata	street	sjö	lake
gränd	lane	slott	castle
hamn	port	stad	city
holme	island	torg	square
kyrka	church	väg	road
ö	island		

Riddarhustorget. This was where the assassin of Gustav III was brutally flogged before being beheaded. On the north side of the square is the classic 17th-century **Riddarhuset** (House of Nobility), Tel. (08) 723 39 00, which is open all year on Monday to Friday between 11:30am and 12:30pm. Arguably Stockholm's most beautiful building, its interior is distinguished by 2,325 coats of arms of noble Swedish families. The original architect, Vallée, a Frenchman, was tragically stabbed to death in a dispute over the building plans, but a German, a Dutchman, and the original architect's son, Jean de la Vallée, finally completed the admirable red-brick and sandstone structure. To this day, members of these noble families can hire the hall for weddings or other such social occasions.

Cross the nearby bridge, Riddarholmsbron, and you will arrive on the island of **Riddarholmen** (Isle of the Nobility). Here, you'll find a former Riksdag (Parliament) building, several palaces, and the copper-topped Birger Jarl's tower, erected by Gustav Vasa in the 16th century. At Riddarholmen quay you get a marvelous view of Lake Mälaren, the heights of Söder (the southern part of Stockholm) and Stadshuset (City Hall) on Kungsholmen (see page 48), which from this vantage point appears to rise straight out of the waters of Lake Mälaren. In the other direction, the shining white hull of the yacht Mälardrottningen lies moored to the quay. Once Barabara Hutton's personal plaything, it is now a hotel and restaurant. It is the elegantly intricate façade, with its tall, distinctive cast-iron latticework spire, of the **Riddarholmskyrkan** (Riddarholm Church; see Highlights, page 79), that dominates this small island. Built in connection with a Franciscan monastery founded by King Magnus Ladulås in 1270, it was completed very early in the 14th century and has been the

A panoramic view from the island of Riddarholmen comprises a number of towering steeples and spires.

burial place of Swedish kings for some 500 years. The interior is a pleasing mix of simplicity and regality; with the walls covered in the coats of arms of the Knights of the Seraphim Order. The floor contains about two hundred graves from different eras. On the anniversary of the death of each knight, the bells of the church are rung resounding as the Seraphim chimes, and his coat of arms is affixed to the wall with two dates — the day he received his order and date of his death. The last regular service was held here in 1807. These days it is only used for memorials and burials.

DJURGÅRDEN

It's easy to see why Stockholmers love Djurgården, which means "Royal Animal Park". This immense, largely unspoiled island of natural beauty used to be a royal hunting park. In addition to miles of woodland trails and magnificent oaks, some of which go back to Viking times, it contains surprising statuary tucked away amidst its greenery, outdoor coffee shops and restaurants, an amusement park, and some of the city's principal museums. Djurgården is perfect for picnicking, jogging, horseback riding, or just enjoying a walk in quiet surroundings. One of the favorite promenades for strollers lies along a path that winds and dips but never strays too far from the shoreline of Djurgårdsbrunnsviken.

Actually, Djurgården consists of two large tracts of land west of the city proper, divided from each other by the east/west axis of **Djurgårdsbrunnviken**, a lovely channel that merges with an even lovelier canal. In the winter, when the water freezes over, people ski or skate on the ice here. To the visitor, this area

While in Stockholm, enjoy a sunny summer day afloat upon the Djurgårdsbrunn Canal.

can be somewhat confusing, as the northern part is shown on maps and guides as Ladugårdsgärdet. Although the TV tower, **Sjöhistoriska Museet** (National Maritime Museum; see page 55) and two other museums are found on this side, they don't attract too many visitors. In fact, the vast majority of visitors to Stockholm will find themselves drawn to the western end of the island actually named Djurgården, to the south. Of the attractions there, three of them are highlights that should not be missed, though the others are worth a visit too.

There is a variety of available transportation here. Most fun, between April and early January, is to take the number 7 tram from Norrmalmstorgm — near Sweden House — and from the same place there also is the option of the number 47 bus. Incidentally, regular tram service was discontinued in 1967 when Sweden switched from left- to right-hand driving, and this line was re-opened as a charity-operated museum line in 1991. It is even possible to take a ferryboat, *Djurgårdsfärjan,* from either Nybroviken or Slussen to the Gröna Lund Tivoli Park. An even better alternative, given fine weather, is to go on foot and return by one of the above suggestions. Start at Nybroplan and follow Strandvägen (Shore Road), a fashionable quayside boulevard in the Östermalm section of town. Whether you choose to walk along the central promenade lined with linden trees or beside the quay where the old schooners are anchored, you'll find this is a pleasant stroll. Keep on Strandvägen until you reach Djurgårdsbron, the bridge to Djurgården.

After crossing the bridge, the huge multi-towered building on your right is the home of the **Nordiska Museet** (see page 55). As impressive as that is, both inside and out, it effectively hides Stockholm's most visited — and a most unique — attraction. Directly behind the Nordiska you will find the **Vasamuseet** (Vasa Museum; see Highlights, page

79), now the permanent home of the early 17th-century man-of-war Vasa warship. Commissioned by King Gustavus II Adolphus on 16 January 1625, it was designed to be the most expensive and richly ornamented naval vessel of its era. However, disaster befell it on its maiden voyage on 10 August 1628 when it capsized and sank in the harbor, soon after being launched. Although its guns were salvaged later that century, the hull lay forgotten until it was discovered in 1956 at a depth of 32 m (105 ft). The next year salvaging operations were begun, but this very complicated process was not completed until 24 April 1961 when the Vasa was sprayed with preservatives, and placed in a temporary museum, Wasavarvet, until 1979. In 1963 divers started combing the seabed and, over the five following seasons, rescued numerous artifacts, including hundreds of sculptures. The vessel made its final voyage in 1988 to this creative new museum at Galärvarvet, which was officially opened by King Carl XVI Gustaf on 15 June 1990.

It's best to begin a visit to the Vasa by watching the introductory film (shown hourly) or by taking a guided tour (offered several times daily). Afterwards, in this open-plan museum, visitors can inspect, but not board, this amazing vessel from observation platforms on seven levels. Of much interest are the exhibition halls housing ornaments and other objects from the ship — pottery, coins, pewter tankards, glassware, clay pipes, cannonballs, and items of clothing taken from the skeletons of 18 Vasa seamen found on the ship. Among the oddest discoveries were a box containing butter — rancid, of course — and a flask of rum, still drinkable after more than three centuries. Children will especially enjoy "sailing" the Vasa using computer simulators.

Just behind the museum, moored on the quayside, is the **Museifartygen** where you can go onboard a steam-powered

The Vasa Museum offers a glimpse into the seafaring history of Scandinavia, as far back as the early 17th century.

1915 icebreaker and a light ship dating from 1903. Between late-May and late-August these can be visited daily from noon to 5pm. The entrance fee is 25kr and the Stockholm Card is valid here.

Following the quayside around the next attraction is the **Aquaria Vattenmuseum** (Aquaria Water Museum), Falkenbergsgatan 2; Tel. (08) 660 49 40, where you will find Nordic and oceanic water environments and a living rain forest. It is open daily mid-June to mid-August from 10am–6pm, and Tuesday–Sunday from 10am–4:30pm at other times. Entrance is 50kr adults and 25kr children; the Stockholm Card is valid.

At Djurgårdsvägen 60, is the **Liljevalchs Konsthall**, Tel. (08) 508 31 330; web site <www.liljevalchs.com>, which mounts excellent exhibitions of paintings, sculpture, and handicrafts. It is open Tuesday–Sunday from 11am–5pm. Entrance is 50kr, and the Stockholm card is valid.

Only a few steps away is **Gröna Lund**, Tel. (08) 587 501 00; web site <www.gronalund.com>, or Tivoli, Stockholm's amusement park. Without the ambiance of the more famous Tivoli in Copenhagen, this still has plenty to make it an attractive stop. In addition to shooting galleries, a merry-go-round, a tunnel of love and numerous restaurants, fast food outlets, and bars, it has a first-rate theater and open-air stage where top Swedish and foreign entertainers perform. It is open between May and September, but the actual hours are rather complicated, so it's best to call ahead. Entrance is 45kr adults and free for children, and it is covered by the Stockholm Card. Admission to the rides costs between 1 to 4 coupons, which can be purchased in discount booklets for 140kr and 210kr, for 16 and 24 coupons respectively.

The array of amusements at Gröna Lund, also known as Tivoli, can fulfill your appetite for fun!

While you're still on this side of Djurgårdsvägen, pause to look at the cluster of old houses on some of the narrow streets near the amusement park. This community, known as **Djurgårdsstaden**, was founded more than 200 years ago and grew up around the Djurgårdsvarvet shipyard.

Now it's time to cross over Djurgårdsvägen to reach the entrance to **Skansen** (see Highlights, page 79), the world's first and most famous open-air museum and a prototype for all the others that followed. Beautifully situated on a 30-hectare (74-acre) hill, it was created by Artur Hazelius in

At Skansen, get a slice of life from across the countryside without ever leaving town.

1891, with the idea of establishing a kind of miniature Sweden, showing how different people, from farmers to aristocrats, lived and worked during different eras.

Some 150 historic buildings from various parts of Sweden constitute an important part of Skansen. They represent a bygone way of life, a culture that started to disappear with the advent of the Industrial Revolution. Gathered here are re-assembled cottages, manor houses, peasant and Lapp huts, and ancient farmsteads, complete with cows, pigs, and other farm animals. Country stores and city shops — including a bakery and an old pharmacy — and the 18th-century Seglora Kyrka, popular for weddings, dot the area. Glassblowers, potters, bookbinders, and goldsmiths are among the crafts-men plying their trade in the workshops.

It also has a very fine zoo featuring northern animals such as reindeer, seals, wolves, deer, bears, and the ever-popular *Älg* (moose) in very natural surroundings, as well as fauna from other parts of the world. Look also for a special children's area, Lill-Skansen, with rabbits, kittens, guinea pigs, and other small animals, along with an aquarium, botanical gardens, indoor and outdoor restaurants, public dance floors, and an open-air stage that features entertainers of international acclaim. There is also an aquarium and a terrarium with exotic animals, al-though this admission price is extra.

It is possible that many visitors to Stockholm may not, initially, feel that Skansen is worth a visit; but overlooking this would be a major mistake. Skansen is an absolute delight. There is always something going on and you can easily spend a whole day or more here without any risk of getting bored. The park is also a pleasant spot to visit in the summer evenings when there are special programs, and the view from the hilltop of the lights of Stockholm (glittering in all directions off the surrounding waters) is spectacular.

Just outside Skansen is the **Biologiska Museet** (Biology Museum; see page 57), which is of much interest in its own right.

There is one more museum on the Djurgården that should not be missed, but it is rather far to walk to. So, jump on a number 7 tram or 47 bus to **Prince Eugen's Waldemarsudde**, Tel. (08) 545 837 00; web site <www.waldemarsudde.com>. This is the former house and art gallery of Prince Eugen, widely known as Sweden's "Painter Prince" and one of the most accomplished landscape painters of his generation. When he died in 1947 at the age of 82, he bequeathed his property to the nation. The public can visit the house — where the ground

Stadhuset (City Hall) has been celebrated for its dramatic architecture and palatial details.

floor offers a fascinating insight into his lifestyle — and the gallery, in a lovely setting of parkland and terraced flower gardens sloping down to a channel of the Baltic Sea.

Waldemarsudde has an ambitious collection of Swedish paintings, mostly from the late 19th and early 20th centuries. There are also more than a hundred works by Prince Eugen. The garden contains a number of first-rate sculptures. Open May–August Tuesday–Sunday from 11am to 5pm, Thursday 11am–8pm; September–April Tuesday, Wednesday, and Friday 11am–4pm and weekends 11am–5pm. Entrance is 50kr, and the Stockholm Card is accepted (see page 125).

STADSHUSET AND OTHER SIGHTS

Most of the major places of interest are found in Stockholm Center, the Old Town, and Djurgården, which have been covered in detail above. However, there are still excellent attractions left to see. Foremost among these is **Stadshuset** (City Hall; see Highlights, page 79), which is located on Kungsholmen island just west of the city center. You can get there by crossing Stadshusbron (City Hall Bridge) from Tegelbacken, just a short walk from Central Station.

When William Butler Yeats came to Stockholm in 1923 to receive the Nobel Prize for Literature, he took a look at the new City Hall and exclaimed that "no work comparable in method and achievement has been accomplished since the Italian cities felt the excitement of the Renaissance..."

Yeats was not alone in lavishing praise on Stockholm's City Hall. Designed by Ragnar Östberg, the building rises gracefully and dramatically from the shore of Lake Mälaren. Artists and craftsmen from all over Sweden contributed to its creation, and it has become a fitting symbol — almost an architectural hymn to the city. Stadshuset is worth several hours of your time, and even then you'll only get an inkling of what went into the construction of this remarkable building. The special hand-cut brick façades; the imposing square tower capped by three golden crowns; the black granite reliefs, pillars, and arches. All miraculously work together to form a unified and coherent whole, a monumental attempt to fuse the many different elements that make up Stockholm. It was inaugurated on Midsummer Day in 1923, the 400th anniversary of Gustav Vasa's coronation on the day he marched into town.

Join one of the guided tours through the handsome interior of City Hall. Highlights include the **Golden Hall**, covered with striking mosaics, the huge glass-domed **Blue Hall** (which is actually red) where the Nobel Prize banquets are held, and the **Prince's Gallery**, with murals executed by Prince Eugen.

The original idea was that all materials used in the construction and decoration were to be Swedish, however the architect was faced with a problem when the French government made a gift of tapestries. He resolved this by placing them in a rather small, round room. Today, this is where Civil weddings are conducted and the happy couples have a choice of two ceremonies; one that lasts three minutes and the other all of 7 seconds!

In a terraced garden by the water lie Carl Eldh's sculptures of the dramatist August Strindberg, the poet Gustaf Fröding, and the painter Ernst Josephson. Also here, on top of a 14 m (46 ft) high column, is Christian Eriksson's bronze statue of Engelbrekt, Sweden's great hero of the Middle Ages.

For a superb view of the Old Town and central Stockholm, if you have the energy, walk to the top of the 115 m (350 ft) tall City Hall Tower.

*All that glitters is gold amidst the ornate mosaics
of the Golden Hall at Stadhuset.*

The artworks displayed at Millesgården represent some of the finest sculpture artists in Sweden.

Extending west of Stadshuset is **Norr Mälarstrand**, a landscaped promenade that follows the water's edge all the way to the **Västerbron** (Western Bridge). This pleasant walk is often crowded with Stockholmers out for a casual stroll, with many parents pushing baby carriages, especially on a sunny Sunday afternoon.

One sight not to be missed is **Millesgården**, Tel. (08) 446 75 90; web site <www.millesgården.se>, the home, studio, and garden of the late Carl Milles (1875–1955), Sweden's famous modern sculptor. Although he lived and worked abroad, mostly in the United States, for long periods, Milles was extremely fond of his place on the island suburb of Lidingö, and managed to spend his summers here.

The gardens, beautifully terraced and overlooking an inlet of the Baltic, provide a superb setting for replicas of Milles' best work. On display are some of his most popular pieces — *Man and Pegasus*, *Europa and the Bull*, and the spectacular *Hand of God*. There is also an important collection of Greek and Roman sculpture, as well as the work of other sculptors. Millesgården itself is a work of art, the creation of a man who worshiped beauty. Silver birch and pine trees stand guard over statues and fountains, rose beds and urns of flowers, marble columns and flights of limestone steps. Carl Milles died at the age of 80 in 1955, and both he and his wife are buried in a small chapel in the garden. Take the underground to Ropsten, then catch a bus or Lidingö local train (one stop) to Torsvik. It is open daily, May–September, from 10am to 5pm and at other times on Tuesday–Sunday from midday to 4pm. Entrance is 60kr, and is covered by the Stockholm Card.

If you have enough time, go over to Söder, the large island on Stockholm's south side, with steep cliffs plunging down into the Baltic and Lake Mälaren. It's a place with a very special atmosphere, quite different from other parts of the city. Söder contains a number of small, closely integrated neighborhoods, clusters of rust-red colored, wooden cottages and artists' studios located in a rural setting.

Start at Slussen (the Sluice Gate), a clover-leafed traffic circle above the narrow canal connecting the lake with the sea. In the summer months, you'll see many pleasure boats lined up here waiting for the canal lock to be opened. Slussen is home, among other things, to one of the city's most curious sights. **Katarinahissen** (The Katarina Lift), Tel. (08) 743 13 95, is open Monday–Saturday 7:30am– 10pm and Sunday 10am–10pm. The fare is 5kr but included on the Stockholm Card. This 100-year-old lift rises in an open shaft to the roof of a tall building, where there is a lovely view of the Old Town from the top. The building is also home to the acclaimed Gondolen restaurant, where diners enjoy fine food and views in equal measure. A walkway at the roof level crosses over to a cliff-top neighborhood of quaint old houses with hidden courtyards.

Now head for **Fjällgatan**, east of the Katarina district, where most of the city sightseeing buses stop. This little street, perched along the edge of a towering ridge overlooking the Baltic, provides the visitor with one of the very best panoramas of Stockholm. Not far from here there is a charming colony of shuttered, fenced-in cottages grouped on the slopes of a grassy hill around the Sofia Kyrka.

To the west of Slussen, there are more picturesque houses at **Mariaberget**. From the heights of Skinnarviksberget, you will experience yet another stunning view of Stockholm, which encompasses sights of Lake Mälaren and Stadshuset.

Once a working-class neighborhood, Slussen has now been somewhat gentrified, and a walk around here will find a surprisingly cosmopolitan and eclectic area with numerous bars, boutiques, and small parks — no major attractions, but nevertheless an attraction in its own right.

☞ MUSEUMS

Stockholm has over 70 museums, with more in the works. A description of major museums, some of special interest cross-referenced in the text, follows below. For more details it is worth obtaining a copy of the informative *Museums in Stockholm* brochure from the tourist office.

Östasiatiska Museet (Museum of Far Eastern Antiquities)

Skeppsholmen; Tel. (08) 519 557 50; web site <www.mfea. se>. Housed in a building dating from 1700, and originally designed as a stable and quarters for Charles XII's bodyguards.

The unmistakable work of Picasso is on display outside of Stockholm's cutting edge Modern Museet.

This enormous collection embraces art from Japan, Korea, India, and China from the Stone Age to the 19th century. Its collection of ancient Chinese art, considered the best in the world outside of China, includes 1,800 objects given to the museum in 1974 by the late King Gustaf VI Adolf, a distinguished archaeologist and a respected authority on Chinese art.

The museum's star exhibits are numerous: ancient Stone Age pottery; a reconstructed Chinese grave furnished with urns and axe heads grouped around a skeleton; colorful ceramics dating from the Ming Dynasty (1368–1644); and a series of highly impressive bronze sacrificial vessels. Open Wednesday–Sunday noon to 5pm and Tuesday noon to 8pm, closed on Monday. Entrance 40kr (see page 29).

Moderna Museet (Museum of Modern Art) *

Skeppsholmen; Tel. (08) 5195 5200; web site <www.modernamuseet.se>. Housing "op," pop, and all kinds of "happenings," this stimulating, trend-setting institution has kept up with the best of contemporary art from the rest of Europe and the United States. It is housed in a stunning new building that opened in 1998 to celebrate Stockholm's role as the 1998 European City of Culture. The museum's extensive collection of 20th-century art includes works by Léger, Matisse, Braque, Modigliani, Klee, and Rauschenberg, as well as by top Swedish artists such as Isaac Grünewald and Bror Hjorth. Open Tuesday–Thursday 11am–8pm and Friday–Sunday 11am–6pm, closed on Monday. Entrance 60kr (see page 29).

Nationalmuseum (National Museum of Fine Arts) *

Sodra Blasieholmen; Tel. (08) 519 543 00; web site <www. nationalmuseum.se>. This is one of the oldest museums in the world. It was founded in 1792, when it occupied a wing of the Royal Palace and was known as the Royal Museum. It moved to its current home, a massively impressive Italian Renaissance-style building, in 1866.

The old masters collection at the Nationalmuseum will surely impress the most worldly museum-goers.

The collection is impressive, and not only because of its size and scope of the paintings, sculptures, decorative arts, drawings and prints. Among the old masters collection you'll find Rembrandts, plus important works by El Greco, Rubens, Goya and Brueghel, and a choice selection of Chardin oils. Courbet, Cézanne, Gauguin, Renoir, and Manet are represented here, as are important Swedish artists, among whom are Carl Larsson, Anders Zorn, and Bruno Liljefors (who is known for his vivid nature studies). Zorn's *Midsummer Dance* is a wonderful evocation of Midsummer's Eve in the province of Dalarna. Other paintings to look for include François Boucher's *The Triumph of Venus*, considered his greatest work, and *The Lady and the Veil* by the Swedish painter Alexander Roslin (1718–1793). In addition to these special treats there are thousands of prints, engravings, and miniatures, more than 200 Russian icons, and a selection of handicrafts to appreciate. Open Tuesday 11am–8pm and Wednesday–Sunday 11am–5pm, closed on Monday. Entrance 60kr (see page 29).

Sjöhistoriska Museet (National Maritime Museum) *

Djurgårdsbrunnsvägen 24; Tel. (08)5195 4900; web site <www.sshm.se/sjohistoriska>. Located in a fine building designed by Ragnar Östberg, architect of the Stadshuset, this interesting museum traces the history of the Swedish navy and the merchant marines. The centerpiece of the collection is the stern of the schooner Amphion, which won a key naval battle against the Russian navy in 1790 under the command of Gustav III. Open daily 10am–5pm, and Tuesday until 8:30pm during school holidays. Entrance 40kr (see page 41).

Nordiska Museet (Nordic Museum) *

Djurgårdsvägen 6-16, Djurgården; Tel. (08) 519 560 00; web site <www.nordm.se>. Housed in one of the most impressive

More palatial than the average museum, the Nordiska Museet has a unique collection of decadent proportions.

buildings in Stockholm, dating from 1907, this museum, illustrating life in Sweden from the 16th century to the present, is the brainchild of Artur Hazelius, creator of Skansen.

Entering the building, you are greeted by Carl Milles' enormous oak statue of Gustav Vasa, father of modern Sweden (see page 16). There is a lot to view here — more than one million objects, in fact. You'll find exhibits depicting the history of upper-class fashions, an interesting section on food and drink with table settings from different periods, and a costume gallery devoted to Swedish peasant dress from the beginning of the 19th century. There's also a feature on the nomadic Lapps and their reindeer and an exhibit concentrating on Nordic folk art that includes Swedish wall paintings, Norwegian tapestries, Finnish drinking vessels, and Danish embroidery. Open Sunday–Tuesday 10am–5pm and until 8pm on Tuesday and Thursday; closed Monday. Entrance 60kr (see page 41).

Biologiska Museet (Museum of Biology) *

Lejonslätten, Djurgården; Tel. (08) 442 82 15; web site <www.skansen.se>. Found just outside Skansen in an Old Norse-style structure completed in 1893 and built for the Stockholm Exhibition of 1897. It was the first museum in the world to consider exhibiting animals in their natural environs. Its creators were two extremely talented men, the taxidermist Gustaf Kolthoff and the painter Bruno Liljefors.

Here you can admire 300 different species of Nordic animals and birds, including polar bears, Arctic wolves, mountain hares and moose, hawk owls, white-tailed eagles, and guillemots nesting on cliffs. They are stuffed, of course, but they look eerily real in these ingeniously constructed settings. The result is an absorbing museum that is sure to fascinate both children and adults. Open daily April–September 10am–4pm and October to March Tuesday–Sunday 10am–3pm. Entrance 20kr (see page 46).

Armémuseum (Army Museum) *

Riddargatan 13; Tel. (08) 7889 95 60; web site <www.armemuseum.org>. Recently renovated and in an interesting building, this museum may not be to everyone's taste. However, as the exhibits are displayed in chronological order it offers a fascinating opportunity to learn about Sweden's complex history. Open Tuesday 11am–8pm and Wednesday–Sunday 11am–4pm; closed Monday. Entrance 60kr.

Historiska Museet (Museum of National Antiquities) *

Narvavägen 13-17 ("T" to Karlaplan); Tel. (08) 519 556 00; web site <www.historiska.se>. Ten thousand years of history unfold eloquently in this excellent museum. Before going inside have a good look at the main entrance. The "door of history," covered with a multitude of allegorical and historical figures in bronze relief, is the work of the renowned Swedish sculptor, Bror Marklund.

The museum has more than 30 rooms, so it's best to pick up a floor plan, available in English. The ground-floor exhibits start with artifacts from the earliest inhabitants of Sweden during the Mesolithic and Neolithic periods. The Viking Age has yielded a rich collection of gold and silver objects, fine examples of ornamental art, and weapons and rune stones from the isle of Gotland. From a slightly earlier epoch, there is the Treasure of Vendel, a remarkable burial site with the dead in their boats surrounded by everyday objects.

Travel back in time as you study the rich and lengthy history of Scandinavia at the Historiska Museet.

There are magnificent examples of medieval church art on the first floor, including wooden crucifixes modeled after Byzantine art, beautifully painted and sculptured altar pieces, baptismal fonts, textile wall hangings, gold chalices, and various processional crosses. One room has been devoted entirely to a reconstruction of a typical medieval country church.

The museum's major new attraction is the Gold Room, located in a "rock chamber" some 7 m (23 ft) below ground level in the museum garden. The circular room displays one of Europe's richest collections of prehistoric jewelry, including gold and silver artifacts dating back as far as AD 400. Open daily, 15 May–14 Sep, 10am–5pm and at other times Tuesday–Sunday 11am–5pm and until 8pm on Thursday. Entrance 60kr.

Musikmuseet (Music Museum) *

Sibyllegatan 2; Tel. (08) 519 554 90; web site <www.musikmuseet.se>. This museum is worth visiting just to see the building that houses it, namely the old Crown Bakery that dates from the mid-17th century, where no bread has been baked since 1958. First opened in 1901, this museum is a music lovers delight with a unique collection of instruments, a folk music section, various workshops and an interactive sound room with high tech and cyber sound. Open Tuesday–Sunday 11am–4pm; closed Monday. Entrance 40kr.

Naturhistoriska riksmuseet (Museum of Natural History) *

Frescativägen 40 ("T" Universitetet); Tel. (08) 519 540 00; web site <www.nrm.se>. This huge museum was established in 1916 and covers various aspects of natural history, including specimens of birds and animals from the Arctic regions. Open daily 10am–6pm and until 8pm on Thursday. Entrance 55kr. The museum's biggest attraction is the new **Cosmonova**, the only IMAX format theater in Sweden and one of the most advanced planetariums in the world. Movies in OMNIMAX, the world's largest format, are on a huge dome screen above the audience. The films shown are mostly documentaries covering subjects like astronauts in space and unusual aspects of life on land and in the oceans. Open daily with shows each hour between 10am and 7pm. Entrance 65kr.

Postmuseum (Postal Museum) *

Lilla Nygatan 6, Gamla Stan; Tel. (08) 781 17 55; web site <www.posten.se/museum>. Documenting the history of the mail service in Sweden from 1636 to the present, the museum contains an excellent philatelic department — in fact, it is one of the largest stamp collections on public view in the world. Among the rarities are the first English stamp cancelled on the day of issue, 6 May 1840. Open Tuesday–Sunday, 11am–4pm; closed Monday. Entrance free.

Strindbergsmuseet (Strindberg Museum) *

Drottninggatan 85; Tel. (08) 411 53 54; web site <www. strindbergsmuseet.se>. The apartment in which Sweden's greatest playwright, August Strindberg, lived during the last years of his life has been reconstructed with authentic furnishings, including his original writing desk. Three adjoining rooms are devoted to his manuscripts, letters, and the photos of actors and actresses who appeared in his plays. Strindberg died in 1912. Open during August Tuesday–Friday 11am–4pm and Saturday/Sunday from noon–4pm; and from September–May open until 7pm on Tuesday. Entrance 30kr.

Tekniska Museet
(National Museum of Science and Technology) *

Museivägen 7; Tel. (08) 450 56 00; web site <www.
tekmu.se>. Bus 69 from Central Station or Sergels Torg.
This museum covers Swedish science and technology
through the ages. One of the more fascinating attractions is a
reconstructed iron ore mine in the basement of the building.
Another highlight is the Royal Model Chamber, displaying
the inventions of Christopher Polhem (1661–751), a genius
often described as the "Father of Swedish Technology."
Open Monday–Friday 10am–4pm and Saturday/Sunday
11am–4pm. Entrance 50kr adults and 20kr for children.

* *Included in the Stockholm Card*

EXCURSIONS

The beauty of its surroundings rival the beauty of Stockholm
itself. To the east are the islands of the archipelago, and to the
west is Lake Mälaren, with a choice collection of castles and
towns at the water's edge.

There are numerous boat excursions all summer long, on
graceful old steamers or fast modern motor launches. Most
of those heading for the archipelago will depart from either
Norra Blasieholmshamnen or Strömkajen, both near the
Grand Hôtel. Stadshusbron, next to the City Hall, is the
departure point for boats around Lake Mälaren.

Stockholm Archipelago

The Swedes call the Stockholm archipelago Skärgården,
which means "garden of skerries", and it's a fitting
description. Huge and infinitely varied, this hauntingly
beautiful archipelago consists of as many as 24,000 rocky
islands of all shapes and sizes, extending for some 48 km (30

Around Stockholm's archipelago, the ancient tradition of sailing is still an important form of local recreation.

miles) into the cold waters of the Baltic. There is nothing like it anywhere else in the world.

In its day the archipelago served as a place of refuge for pirates and smugglers. Later, fishermen lived in unpainted wooden shacks and wealthy noblemen built great estates on many of the islands. In this century the archipelago has become the favorite playground of Stockholmers that visit their summer holiday houses on weekends or for longer vacations. They sail, fish, swim, and sun themselves on the smooth boulders by the water. The archipelago is divided into three distinct sections, each with its own character and special atmosphere. The inner group is made up of larger islands covered with forests and farmland. The middle archipelago consists of a jumble of large and small islands, some with woods and fields of wildflowers, separated by a labyrinth of narrow channels and sounds. The outer archipelago, mostly uninhabited, is a barren seascape of desolate rock islands.

Vaxholm is an attractive waterfront town in the inner archipelago, reached by way of a charming, 40-minute or so, cruise aboard one of the two early 20th-century classic Vaxholm boats operated by Strömma Kanalbolaget, Tel. (08) 587 140 10; web site <www.strommakanalbolaget.com>. These set sail from Nybroplan for a fare of 110kr, and it is worth considering having lunch aboard. Vaxholm's chief attraction is the 16th-century **Fästnings Museet** (Vaxholm Fortress Museum; Tel. (08) 541 721 57). On a little island guarding the straits by Vaxholm, this foreboding 16th-century fortress is now the National Museum of Coastal Defense. Open daily, 29 May–29 Aug, from midday–4pm. Entrance 30kr. Vaxholm is a charming place, with waterside walking paths. From the harbor you can watch the motorboats and sailboats maneuvering through the narrow channel as they head for more distant points in the Stockholm archipelago.

Take a trip to a fortress — the monolithic structure at Vaxholm actually houses an interesting museum.

Sandhamn is located on a Baltic island at the outer edge of the archipelago. The fastest way there is on a Cinderella Båtarna vessel, Tel. (08) 587 140 50; web site <www.cinderellabatarna.com> from Strandvågen; 95kr one way. Plan a return on the Strömma Kanalbolaget canal trip, which takes 3 hours and also costs 95kr one way. In both circumstances, there is a restaurant/bar on board and you will be able to take in all the diverse and dramatic elements that make up this stunning island world. An important pilot station since the end of the 17th century, Sandhamn is a yachting center and home of the fashionable Royal Swedish Yacht Club. The tiny, charming village has only about 100 year-round residents, but the figure swells in the summer when tourists and Stockholmers who have summer holiday cottages here invade the island. Sandhamn's summer

If hobnobbing with the upper-class yacht foks is your cup of tea, don't miss a visit to Sandhamn.

amenities include several hotels, an old inn, a restaurant with dancing, and good swimming and sailing facilities. In July Sandhamn hosts an international regatta.

If you prefer not to venture so far into the archipelago, then a trip to the **Feather Islands** is for you. Numerous attractions await along with restaurants, bars and even a handicraft village where you can purchase souvenirs. Strömma Kanalbolaget operates frequent sailings from Nybroplan, a return ticket costs 65kr.

Another fine outing is a cruise to **Mariehamn**, the capital of the Åland islands, comprised of 9,970 sq km (3,850 sq miles) of bays, inlets, islands, and skerries located about midway between Sweden and Finland. This autonomous province of Finland has a population of 25,000, most of whom also speak Swedish.

Day cruises, although an overnight stop is better, leave in the morning, stop for a couple of hours in Mariehamn, and are back in Stockholm by late evening. You can also take a 24-hour excursion, sleeping onboard in a comfortable cabin or spending the night in a hotel in Mariehamn. The town has good accommodation facilities and a number of excellent restaurants.

Travelers on these cruise ships will enjoy a sumptuous smörgåsbord, and the bars, dance lounges, and nightclubs onboard are always lively. Tax-free prices make drinks during the journey inexpensive, and since the ships pass through the Stockholm archipelago, you will enjoy a scenic feast as well. For more details, contact the Ålandsbutiken shop in Sweden House, Tel. (08) 21 05 15; fax (08) 21 01 25; web site <www.alandsbutiken.se>.

Lake Mälaren

Mälaren is the country's third largest lake, stretching more than 110 km (68 miles) west of Stockholm. This area, the

Lake Mälaren Valley, has been justly termed the cradle of Swedish civilization and its most important historic sights are within easy traveling distance from the city via waterways.

An absolute must, and a most pleasant and rewarding experience, is an excursion to Drottningholm Palace, situated on a small island in an inlet of Lake Mälaren. A Strömma Kanalbolaget boat that departs and returns frequently from Stadshusbron will take you through a beautiful stretch of Mälaren and get you there in under an hour. A French-style palace built in the late 17th century and described as the Versailles of Sweden, **Drottningholm**, (see Outside Stockholm Highlights, page 80), is now the home of the royal family, who live in the south wing (not open to the public). But don't worry, what you can see is well worth it. This is one of those palaces that actually looks and feels like a royal palace; gilded, sumptuous, and very regal indeed, especially Hedvig Eleonora's State Bedchamber — considered the most expensive Baroque interior in Sweden. Equally impressive are the library and richly decorated staircase.

Drottningholm is a multifaceted attraction. Its extensive gardens, formal in the French style with statuary, fountains, trees, are a delight to walk around. Hidden away to the left of the formal gardens are two very different and very unusual places. The **Kina Slott** Chinese Pavilion, Tel. (08) 402 62 70, an unusual combination of the Rococo and Chinese styles with its two curved wings, is a real anomaly. In fact, when it was designed, no one had any real idea of what a Chinese Pavilion should look like, and as a consequence, this is just a conceptualization. It was commissioned by King Adolf Fredrik as a surprise gift to his wife, Queen Lovisa Ulrika, on her birthday in 1753. After a complete renovation between 1989 and 1996, it can now be seen in its original state. Open daily, May–August, 11am–4:30pm, September noon–3:30pm,

On Lake Mälaren, the elaborate Drottingholm Palace has all the magnificence you would expect from a royal home.

and April and October 1pm–3:30pm. Guided tours mid-June to end of August at 11am, noon, 2pm, and 3pm and in September at noon and 2pm. Entrance 50kr, included on the Stockholm Card. Very close to it is the even more unusual **Guard's Tent**. Well, it does look just like a tent, but a close-up look tells you something different. In fact, it was built in 1781 to serve as quarters for the dragoons of Gustav III, and the intent was to make it look like a "tent in a Turkish army camp." Open mid-June to mid-August (closed 24 June) noon–4pm. Entrance free.

The **Drottningholm Court Theatre**, Tel. (08) 759 04 06; web site <www.drottningholmsteatern.dtm.se>, is adjacent to the palace and is one of the world's most famous theatrical establishments. Dating from the 18th century, this is the oldest theater in the world in its original state — with the stage machinery still in use. Except for the stage lighting — electricity has replaced candlelight — nothing has changed since King Gustav III, the patron of the arts, attended opera performances here. During the summer, this gem of a theater is the venue for operas by Handel, Gluck, Mozart, and others, as well as ballet. The additional touch of musicians dressed up in authentic period costumes and wearing powdered wigs makes you feel as if you're attending a court entertainment some 200 years ago. Before or after the performance, take the opportunity to look at the collections of pictures and costumes tracing the history of stage art, exhibited in the rooms around the auditorium. They include rare Italian and French theatrical designs from the 16th to the 18th centuries and original sketches by Gustav III's stage painter. Even if you can't make a performance, then a guided

Björkö is one of the lovely islands that is only a stone's throw — really a short boat ride — from Stockholm.

tour is a must. During May they are at 12:30pm, 1:30pm, 2:30pm, 3:30pm and 4:30pm. Between June and August (except 23 June), there are extra tours at 11am and 11:30am. In September, there are only tours at 1:30pm, 2:30pm, and 3:30pm. Entrance is 50kr, included on the Stockholm Card.

A trip to Björkö (Birch Island), one of the lake's 300 islands, should also be considered. This was the site of **Birka**, Sweden's earliest trading center, where Sweden's first contacts with Christianity were made in the 9th century. Here St. Ansgar built a church and preached to the heathens in the year 830. Obliterated in the 11th century, all that remains of the once-flourishing town of Birka are the faint traces of old fortifications and around 3,000 Viking graves. The island is a pleasant, relaxing place to spend part of a day. You can reach Björkö in slightly less than 2-hours on a Strömma Kanalbolaget boat that departs and returns from Stadshusbron in the summer months.

A site that justifies a full day's excursion is **Gripsholm Castle**, another of Lake Mälaren's outstanding attractions. You can be there in an hour and a half by train to Läggesta, followed by a short bus ride. An alternative route by boat, however, is a far more pleasing proposition. The SS Mariefred, Tel. (08) 669 88 50; web site <www.gmaa.se>, is a coal-fired steamer that has been plying the same route since 1903. It makes for a highly memorable trip and you can even enjoy a tasty dinner on board. It departs from Stadshusbron, in the summer, at 10:30, and returns from Mariefred at 4:30pm, with each trip taking three and a half hours.

At journey's end you'll see the massive, turreted bulk of Gripsholm Slott's Gripsholm Castle (see Outside Stockholm Highlights, page 80), mirrored like a stage set in the waters of the lake. There was a castle on this site in the 1300s, built by the great Bo Jonsson Grip, but the present structure was built by Gustav Vasa in the 1530s — and subsequently added on to and modified by nearly every succeeding Swedish monarch. The castle served as a state prison at one time, and the deposed King Erik XIV was held captive in its tower. Now a museum, Gripsholm houses one of the largest collections of historical portraits in the world. Don't miss the small castle theater built by Gustav III (who was also responsible for the Drottningholm Theatre), or the two 16th-century bronze cannons in the outer courtyard, seized in wars with the Russians.

Next door to the castle is **Mariefred**, where the steamer to Gripsholm docks. You may want to pause a while in this attractive little town of yellow and red frame houses, with lovely gardens lined up in tight rows beside narrow streets and a cobblestone square. A white Baroque church and an 18th-century town hall are two of the highlights.

Before leaving Mariefred you should take a ride on the **Östra Södermanlands Järnväg** (East Södermanland Railway), a rolling museum of vintage coaches pulled by an old steam engine. This narrow-gauge railway, which dates from 1895, is maintained by local rail buffs. It runs from Mariefred to Läggesta, a distance of 4 km (2½ miles). At a top speed of 11 km/h (7 mph), it's a slow but delightful trip.

Two other places merit consideration for full day trips. Of these, the closest to Stockholm is **Sigtuna**, situated on a beautiful, slender arm of the lake. Sigtuna, most probably Sweden's oldest town, was founded in 980 by Olof Skötkonung, the country's first Christian king. It served as the religious center of the country — a role later taken over by Uppsala — and is the site of some of Sweden's oldest churches. It was also Sweden's first capital and a lively trading port until a series of disasters struck. First, Estonian pirates raided Sigtuna and burned it to the ground. The town gradually recovered, but Gustav Vasa, fired by the ideas of the Reformation, shut down its monasteries. The monks left and the town fell into obscurity.

Today Sigtuna is a lakeside idyll with the ruins of four churches, built between 1060 and 1130. Mariakyrkan (St. Mary's), is a monastery church of the 13th century, and remains as mute testimony to Sigtuna's glorious past. Walk along Storgatan, said to be the oldest street in Sweden, and have a look at the quaint, toy-like town hall, dating from 1744. Other points of interest, aside from the church ruins and scat-

Sigtuna is likely to be Sweden's oldest town, thanks to founder Olof, now a saint.

tered rune stones from the Viking era, are the Fornhemmet Museum, containing local archaeological finds, and the Lundström House, a good example of late 19th-century architecture filled with furniture from the same period. The Sigtuna Foundation, an important religious institution, recently injected new life into the town. It has played host to many prominent authors and scholars who have come here to put the finishing touches on a book or dissertation in the guest rooms that overlook a cloister and rose garden.

Skoklosters Slott (Skokloster Castle), Tel. (018) 38 60 77, is a magnificent Baroque palace on the edge of a lovely bay of Lake Mälaren, about 20 km (12 miles) northeast of

Sigtuna. It was constructed in the latter part of the 17th century by Carl Gustaf Wrangel, a field marshal under Gustavus Adolphus in the Thirty Years' War. The castle's 100 oversized rooms house a fabulous collection of historical treasures, mostly from the 17th century when Sweden was Europe's preeminent military power. The collection includes silver and glass pieces, tapestries, Baroque furniture, over 1,000 paintings, and 20,000 rare books and manuscripts, much of it war booty. The arms collection, one of the largest in the world, begins with crossbows and includes such oddities as a set of executioner's swords and a 2½ m- (8 ft-) long rifle that belonged to Queen Kristina. There are daily guided tours of the castle, between May and August, every hour between 11am–4pm; in April, September, and October Monday–Friday at 1pm and Saturday/Sunday at 1pm, 2pm, and 3pm. It is closed between November and March. Skokloster's vast estate also has a restaurant, a modern hotel, and a Motor Museum, with a fine collection of vintage and veteran cars and engines. The prize exhibits are an 1899 Renault, an elegant maroon 1911 Austin, and a Spitfire engine from the time of the Battle of Britain.

Although there are other methods of reaching Sigtuna and Skokloster, the most pleasant and relaxing is by way of a Strömma Kanalbolaget boat. It leaves Stadshusbron at 9:45am and arrives at Sigtuna at 12:15pm and Skokloster at 1:10pm, returning from Skokloster at 3:40pm and Sigtuna at 4:30pm and arriving back in Stockholm at 7pm. The fare is 140kr (165kr return), and a meal on the boat is very enjoyable indeed.

Uppsala

Uppsala, population 165,000, is 73 km (45 miles) north of Stockholm and can be reached in just 40 minutes by train from Centralstationen. This excursion can justify an overnight stop.

History jostles you at virtually every corner in Uppsala, an ancient center of culture, religion, and education. It's the seat of the Archbishop of the Swedish Church and home of Uppsala University, one of the world's great institutions of higher learning, which celebrated its 500th anniversary in 1977. It also has a charming ambiance, with the Fyrisån river meandering its way through the center of town, green patina forming on the campus statues, rare and beautiful flowers blooming in the Linnaeus Gardens, and the old wooden buildings aging gracefully and in sharp contrast to the new glass and steel structures. Most distinctive of all is Uppsala's skyline silhouette; the twin spires of the cathedral and the round towers of the castle are both centuries-old landmarks that dominate the city.

A stop at the Uppsala Tourist Office, Fyristorg 8; Tel. (018) 27 48 00; fax (018) 13 28 95; or web site <www.uppsala. se>, will arm you with all the necessary information you will need before you set out to explore the town.

Begin your sightseeing at **Uppsala Domkyrka** (Uppsala Cathedral; see Outside Stockholm Highlights, page 80), right in the middle of the university grounds. This mas-

The picture postcard spires of Uppsala Domkyrka are striking against the blue sky.

sive 13th-century cathedral with its lofty 122 m (400 ft) tall spires was completed over a span of 150 years. Many famous Swedes are buried here: King Gustav Vasa (and his three wives); St. Erik — Sweden's patron saint and king who died a martyr in Uppsala in 1160; Emanuel Swedenborg, mystic, scientist, and philosopher; and Carl Linnaeus, the botanist who, like Swedenborg, worked at Uppsala University. The Treasury Tower Museum contains religious tapestries, articles of silver and gold, and other objects of great historical and aesthetic interest. It is open Monday–Saturday 10am–5pm and Sunday 12:30pm–5pm. Entrance fee is 20kr.

Pause to look at the medieval wall paintings in the **Trinity Church** (Helga Trefaldighetskyrkan) nearby before you head off for the **Uppsala Slott** (castle), the cathedral's secular rival. Construction of this looming red structure, on a hill overlooking the town, began in the 1540s under Gustav Vasa. Having severed ties with the pope, the king intended the castle to be a symbol of royal power; the cannons were, therefore, aimed directly at the archbishop's residence. The castle has been the setting of lavish coronation feasts and many dramatic historic events. It was here, for instance, that Gustavus Adolphus held the talks that led Sweden into the Thirty Years' War, and that Queen Kristina gave up her crown in 1654 before setting off for Rome. Today Uppsala Castle is home to the Uppsala Konstmuseum (Uppsala Art Museum), Tel. (018) 27 24 82; web site <www.uppsala.se/konstmuseum>, which exhibits contemporary art in these historic surroundings. Open Tuesday–Friday noon–4pm and Saturday/Sunday 11am–5pm. Entrance fee is 20kr.

Of the university buildings, the most notable is **Carolina Rediviva**, Dag Hammarskjöldsväg 1; Tel. (018) 471 39 00; web site <www.ub.uu.se>, which houses the biggest and oldest library in Sweden, founded by Gustavus Adolphus in the 17th century. The collection contains more than two million books and half a million manuscripts and documents, many from medieval times. Among them are extremely rare items, including the Codex Argenteus (Gothic Silver Bible), written in the sixth century in silver letters and gold capitals on purple parchment. Open mid-June to mid-August, Monday–Friday 9am–5pm, Saturday 10am–5pm and Sunday 11am–4pm, and from mid-August to mid-September it opens until 8pm during the week, closes at 4pm on Saturday and Sunday.

Drop into the **Gustavianum**, Akademigatan 3; Tel. (018) 471 75 71; web site <www. gustavianum.uu.se>, a university building topped by a most curious room; an octagonal anatomical theater under a striking dome. It was constructed in 1662 by Olof Rudbeck, one of the many brilliant scientists who have taught and conducted research here. He used the room to dissect bodies for medical instruction. The Gustavianum opens daily between mid-June and mid-August, from 11am–4pm, but remains open until 8pm on Thursdays. Entrance fee is 40kr.

Many people travel to Uppsala with one purpose in mind: to visit places connected with Carl Linnaeus, well known throughout the world as the "Father of Modern Botany" and also as the "Flower King." Linnaeus came to Uppsala in 1728 as a medical student, was appointed lecturer in botany after only two years at the university, and became a professor of medicine in 1741. In his lifetime Linnaeus named and described some 10,000 different species of plants.

Some of these species can be seen in the university's **Linnéträdgården,** Svartbäcksgatan 27; Tel. (018) 10 94 90; web site <www.linnaeus.uu.se>, which houses 1,300 plants arranged according to species, exactly as they were in Linnaeus's era. His home in the gardens is now a museum and is open to the public. The gardens are open daily between May and August from 9am–9pm and September 9am–7pm with an entrance fee of 20kr. The museum is open between June and mid-September on Tuesday–Sunday from noon–4pm.

During the summer months, botanists lead groups of visitors on walks along three marked trails following the footsteps of Linnaeus in the forests around Uppsala. You can also visit **Hammarby**, Linnaeus's summer home 13 km (8 miles) from Uppsala, where he received hundreds of students from all over the world. The garden here is said to contain a number of specimens planted by Linnaeus himself. This is open daily May–September, from 8am–8pm. Entrance fee is 20kr.

Continuing on with this theme, the **Botaniska trädgården** (Botanical Garden), Villavägen 6-8; Tel. (018) 471 28 38; web site <www.botan.uu.se>, is a must-see for those with such interests. The oldest part, Baroque in style, dates back to the mid-17th century. Altogether, over 13,000 different species and sub species from around the world are found here, including tropical plants, Mediterranean trees, and shrubs in the Tropical Greenhouse and Orangery. The gardens are open daily 7am–8:30pm, closing at 7pm between October and April. The Tropical Greenhouse opens May–September, Monday–Thursday 9:30am–2:30pm and Saturday noon–3pm, and March–October on Sunday noon–3pm. The Orangery is open Monday–Thursday 9:30am–3:30pm and Friday 9:30am–2:30pm. Entrance to the gardens is free and is 20kr each for the Tropical Greenhouse and Orangery.

Be sure to make the excursion to **Gamla Uppsala** (Old Uppsala), Tel. (018) 23 93 00; web site <www.raa.se /gamlauppsala>, about 3 km (2 miles) out of town and reached by regular bus service from the city center. This is the site of the ruins of a pagan temple and three huge burial mounds said to contain the remains of kings mentioned in the epic *Beowulf*. The graves, dating from the 6th century, are called Kungshögarna (Kings' Hills). A medieval parish church stands solidly on the remnants of the heathen temple where blood once flowed profusely as human and animal sacrifices were offered up to the gods. The historical center is open daily mid-May–mid-August, from 10am–5pm and late August–September from 10am–4pm. Entrance fee is 50kr. The church is open daily from 9am–6pm; entrance free. Close by is the Odinsburg Inn, where you can drink mead (*mjöd*) from old Viking ox-horns at a restaurant open noon–6pm, or the café (open from 10am–6pm).

Fans of the epic **Beowulf** *might want to make an excursion to Gamla Uppsala.*

While Uppsala is a tranquil place most of the year, there is one special occasion when suppressed emotions virtually explode. This takes place on Walpurgis Night, in tradition a half-pagan, half-Christian celebration, held on the last day of April. The ceremony begins in the afternoon, when undergraduates and friends gather in front of the Carolina Rediviva and, at a signal from the rector of the university, let out a huge cheer before donning their white student caps. The celebration goes on into the evening, when the whole university — students, professors, and alumni — march with flaming torches and flags of the "nations" (that is, student clubs representing different Swedish provinces) to the summit of the castle hill. Here they burst into songs hailing the country and the arrival of spring. The festivities continue at the student clubs until the early hours of the morning.

Highlights

Hallwylska Museet (Hallwyl Collection) * Hamngatan 4; Tel. (08) 519 555 99; web site <www.lsh.se>. This distinguished private palace, dating from 1898, is full of amazingly valuable collections and original decorations. Guided tours in English daily from 21 Jun–15 Aug at 1pm, and at 1pm on Sunday the rest of the year. Entrance 60kr (see page 27).

Kungliga Slottet (Royal Palace) * Tel. (08) 402 61 30; web site <www.royalcourt.se>. In Gamla Stan, this official residence of the King is a majestic 18th-century structure that includes the Royal Apartments, Hall of State, Gustav III's Museum of Antiquities, Treasury, Royal Chapel, and Tre Kronor Museum. Open daily May–Aug 10am–4pm, and Sep–Apr Tue–Sun noon–3pm. The Royal Chapel is open May–Aug, 10am–4pm, and Sep–April; Sunday church service at 11am. Combination ticket for all parts of the palace 100kr and free admission to Royal Chapel, with free guided tours (see page 32).

Livrustkammaren (Royal Armoury) * Slottsbacken 3 by Royal Palace; Tel. (08) 519 555 44; web site <www.lsh.se>. This has fascinating exhibits tracing the history of the country's monarchs from Gustav Vasa to date. Open daily Jun–Aug, 10am–5pm and until 8pm on Thu (except 1 Jun to 31 Aug). Daily Sep–May, from 11am–5pm and until 8pm on Thu. Guided tours in English (26 Jun to 3 Sept Mon–Fri at 1pm and Sat and Sun 2pm). Entrance 60kr (see page 33)

Changing the Guard at Royal Palace Tel. (08) 402 63 17; web site <www.hogvakten.mil.se>. A favorite attraction, with a military band that marches through the city. In June and August, watch the change Mon–Sat 12:15pm, Sundays and holidays at 1:15pm; April–Oct Wednesday and Saturday at

12:15pm, Sundays and holidays at 1:15pm (except for Christmas Eve and New Year's Eve, when it is a 12:15pm show). November–March has Wednesday and Saturday shows at noon, but these only occasionally have music. The show is free of charge (see page 34).

Riddarholmskyrkan (Riddarholm Church) * Riddarholmen; Tel. (08) 402 61 30; web site <www.royalcourt.se>. With an elaborate exterior and regal, simple interior this has been the burial place for Swedish royalty for some 500 years. Open daily May–August, 10am–4pm and September on Saturday/Sunday noon–3pm. Entrance 20kr (see page 38).

Vasamuseet (The Vasa Museum) * Galärvarvsvägen, 14, Djurgården; Tel. (08) 519 548 00; web site <www.vasamuseet.se>. Architecturally bold, this holds the hull of a 1628 man-of-war. Open daily, 10 Jun–20 Aug, from 9:30am to 7pm, and 21 Aug–9 Jun, from 10am–5pm and until 8pm on Wed. Entrance 60kr (see page 41).

Skansen * Djurgården; Tel. (08) 442 80 00; web site <www.skansen.se>. Vast open-air museum representing traditional ways of life in Sweden. Includes historic buildings, herb garden, zoo, aquarium and open-air theater. Open daily, Jun–Aug, 10am–10pm, Sep–Apr, 10am–4pm and May 10am–8pm. Entrance 30–60kr (see page 45).

Stadshuset (City Hall) * Hantverkargartan 1; Tel. (08) 508 290 59. Imposing landmark, site of the annual Nobel Prize celebrations and dinner, and a huge tower with views over the city. Guided tours in English, Jun–Aug, 10am, 11am, noon, and 2pm; Sept 10am, noon, and 2pm; and Oct–May 10am and noon. Entrance 40kr (see page 48).

* Included on the Stockholm Card.

Outside Stockholm Highlights

Drottningholms Slott (Drottningholm Palace) * Lake Mälaren; Tel. (08) 402 62 80; web site <www.royalcourt.se>. The home of the Royal Family (in a wing), this beautiful palace was built in 1662 and is Sweden's version of Versailles. This estate has been declared a World Heritage Site by UNESCO. Open daily May–Aug, 10am–4:30pm and Sept noon to 3:30pm and, Oct to Apr, on Sat/Sun noon–3:30pm. There are guided tours in English in May to early June on Saturday and Sunday at 11am, 12pm, 1pm, and 3pm; from early June–August they are every day at the same times; in September daily at noon and 2pm; and October–April on Saturday and Sunday at 12pm, 1pm, and 2pm. Entrance 50kr; gardens free (see page 66).

Gripsholms Slott (Gripsholm Castle) * Gripsholm Mariefred; Tel. (0159) 101 94; web site <www.royalcourt. se>. An imposing and attractive royal castle constructed by the Vasa kings in the 16th century. Open daily May–Aug, from 10am–4pm, on Tuesday–Sunday in September from 10am to 3pm and on Sat/Sun, Oct–Apr, from noom–3pm. Entrance 50kr (see page 69).

Uppsala Domkyrka (Uppsala Cathedral) Uppsala; Tel. (018) 18 72 01. Scandinavia's largest church, work started on this site in 1260 and it was consecrated in 1435. From then until the 18th century Swedish monarchs were crowned here. It holds numerous tombs and is the National Temple of the Church of Sweden, the archdiocese, and a parish church. Look for the 16th-century golden shrine, Baroque pulpit, and modern textiles. Open daily 8am–6pm, with guided tours from mid-June to the end of August (see page 73).

*** Included on the Stockholm Card**

WHAT TO DO

SHOPPING

Shopping in Stockholm is a delightful experience, an entry into a very special world of design. The best-known products are those of the industrial arts and handicrafts, such as glassware, ceramics, stainless-steel cutlery, silver, furniture, and textiles. Sweden's fine reputation in these fields rests on old traditions of skilled craftsmanship passed down through the generations. Contemporary Swedish design has its roots in the peasant art of the past.

You'll find a broad range of shops and department stores in Stockholm, many of which are themselves very beautiful. English is widely spoken.

Most Stockholm shops open from 10am to 6pm on weekdays, but close early on Saturday, between 1pm and 4pm. Department stores stay open later on certain days and may also open on Sundays.

Value-Added Tax Refunds

V.A.T., or sales tax (called Moms in Sweden), is 25% on all products (and on most services). However, there is a way to avoid this tax, whereby Moms will be refunded in cash at any point of departure to visitors who buy in shops displaying the blue-and-yellow "Tax-Free Shopping" sticker. You need to present your passport at the time of purchase. Later, you simply hand over the tax-free shopping form provided by the shop (be sure to fill out the back) at the tax-free service counter in ports and airports and on ships. Note that refunds apply for a limited period after purchase, and are only available to those who are not residents of Scandinavia.

Where to Shop

There are three large department stores in the center. One is PUB, on the corner of Drottninggatan and Kungsgatan, a half block from Hötorget. The open-air market at Hötorget makes this a good place to start a shopping tour.

From PUB, work your way south along Drottninggatan to Åhléns department store and Sergels Torg. An underground shopping mall then brings you directly to the basement of NK, Stockholm's classic department store. Head east from NK along Hamngatan until you come to Norrmalmstorg. Turn left into Biblioteksgatan, a short, car-free street which will take you to Stureplan. Then head west along broad Kungsgatan and you'll soon be back to the starting point.

For fun shopping in a medieval milieu, try exploring Gamla Stan. Västerlånggatan, the pedestrian street bisecting the island, is lined with shops and restaurants. You'll find smaller shops and boutiques among the lanes that branch off Västerlånggatan.

The gift shop in the Royal Palace is worth visiting for its array of unusual souvenirs.

Stockholm's main markets are the colorful Östermalmstorg, an indoor market noted for its cheese and fish specialities, and Hötorget, a lively outdoor market where the locals buy their food from Monday to Saturday and shop for crafts on Sunday.

Good Buys

Glassware. This is Sweden's most famous design product, and one of the most popular souvenir items. Names such as Orrefors, Kosta, and Boda are recognized around the world, and talented artists and artisans working for these, and other companies, consistently produce inventive and creative designs.

However, it is expensive even here. Look for special sale items and have the company ship your purchases back for you — it's a little more expensive, but safer.

Ceramics. Rörstrand and Gustavsberg are the predominant names in this field, but there are many smaller companies. Here again there is a wide choice, ranging from charming and fanciful items that easily fit your suitcase and wallet to one-of-a-kind sculptures with a price tag to match their considerable size.

If you are visiting a ceramic factory, you may find something suitable that is priced below what you would have to pay in a shop.

The department store NK offers great shopping for just about anything you may want.

Home furnishings. Like the other Scandinavian countries, Sweden is famous for it emphasis on design — especially on products for the home and furniture. Svenskt Tenn, Strandvägen 5, Tel. (08) 670 16 00; web site <www.svenskttenn.se>, is one of the best stores to find such items in Stockholm.

Stainless tableware. This is another superb national product that has won international recognition. Swedish cutlery, or flatware, is not only beautiful, but makes a fine gift that is easy to carry home.

Souvenirs. Brightly painted, red, hand-carved Dala horses, named after the province of Dalarna where they originated, are probably the most typical, and popular, of Swedish souvenirs. Other such typical souvenirs are painted linen tapestries, sweaters and other knitwear, and beautiful handmade dolls. There are numerous souvenir shops selling these types of items, but Svensk Hemslöjd (The Swedish Handicraft Society), Sveavägen 44 (by Hötorget), Tel. (08) 23 21 15; web site <www.svenskhemslojd.com>, is the only store that offers a selection of genuine Swedish handicrafts from the entire country. Kilgren Knives & Clothing, Västerlånggatan 45, Tel. (08) 20 46 80; web site <www.kilgren.aos.se>, in Gamla Stan, offers a range of Swedish-designed knitwear and the largest selection of knives in Stockholm.

Lapp handicrafts. Although Stockholm is far from Lappland, which extends beyond the Arctic Circle, many stores sell a range of knife handles, buckles, pouches, and other goods handcrafted out of reindeer antlers and skins.

Suede. Coats, jackets, and even skirts made out of suede are excellent buys in Stockholm. Suede, in fact, is a Swedish invention, and also is the French word for Sweden.

Silver. Silversmiths such as Sigurd Persson continue to turn out bold and innovative necklaces, bracelets, and rings. They also fashion stunning silver bowls, cigarette cases, and the like.

Clogs. These traditional wooden Swedish shoes, called träskor, have become popular in many parts of the world. They are available in Stockholm's shops in a wide range of designs.

Cameras. These are a particularly good buy in Sweden, and include Hasselblad, the Swedish camera used in space by American astronauts.

Sporting goods. The Swedes, being such keen campers, are renowned for their excellent camping equipment, as well as the fishing rods and reels made by ABU, a Swedish company that has become one of the world's biggest exporters of high-quality fishing gear.

Candles. Swedes create a cozy mood during the long winter nights by using candles to light their homes. You'll find them sold in all imaginable sizes, shapes, and colors. The variety of candlesticks — in all kinds of materials from glass and metal to wood and straw — is equally broad.

Christmas decorations. For Swedes, Christmas is a time of strong tradition, and the Yuletide ornaments are frequently very attractive. Larger department stores, having realized the decorations' potential as souvenirs, are today offering tourists a small selection of these splendid holiday items all year round.

Typical Swedish handicrafts like these can be found at the glassworks at Skansen.

Food. Just before you leave Stockholm, don't forget to buy a selection of Swedish cheese, herring, caviar, smoked salmon, crispbread, and — last but not least — a bottle of aquavit, the popular throat-burning national drink, so that you can entertain your friends back home with a little smörgåsbord.

ENTERTAINMENT

No one would claim that the entertainment possibilities in Stockholm are equal to those of, say, New York or London. However, enough goes on in this town to satisfy the desires of any visitor. Moreover, the long, light Stockholm summer nights are made-to-order for pleasurable outdoor activities. An indispensable guide to what's happening in the city, *What's On*, is published monthly by the Stockholm Information Service, and is available free at your hotel and many other places.

Music and Theater

The massive auditorium of the Stockholm Konserthuset is the main venue for serious music during the winter months, the season stretching from September to May or June. In summer you can enjoy concerts in the many splendid settings scattered throughout the Stockholm area — the Royal Palace, the courtyard of the Hallwylska Museet, Prince Eugen's Waldemarsudde, St. Jacob's Church, and the German Church in the Old Town. There

Join the music lovers that come out to this lovely setting at Riddarholmen for a concert on a summer evening.

are also open-air concerts in many of the city parks, including Kungsträdgarden in the heart of town.

First-rate opera and ballet are offered at Operan (Royal Opera) from early autumn to late spring. In summer the Drottningholm Court Theatre (see page 67) stages 17th- and 18th-century drama. Check to see if the Cullberg Ballet Company, formed by the choreographer Birgit Cullberg, is performing during your stay in Stockholm.

Modern and classical plays are staged at Kungliga Dramatiska Teatern and Stadsteatern (Stockholm Municipal Theater), though in Swedish only. The Marionette Theater mounts puppet and marionette productions suitable for children and adults.

There are many cinemas in the city center, and many foreign films are shown in their original language with Swedish subtitles. Check the evening newspapers to see what's playing.

Top spots for jazz are the Stampen, a pub in the Old Town, and the Lydmar Hotel. The Stockholm Jazz and Blues Festival is held during the last weekend in June and the first weekend in July on Skeppsholmen.

Nightlife

Night-owls will be pleased that the sidewalks in Stockholm are no longer rolled up at midnight. Many of the nightclubs, including a few at hotels, now stay open until 3am or later. All have live dance music; some also offer cabaret and variety shows. If you sit at a table you are expected to eat, but at the bar ordering food is unnecessary. There are also dance restaurants in town that close earlier, at around 1am. Unattached males and unescorted females tend to be the usual patrons of Stockholm dance restaurants and nightclubs, so these are good places to meet people.

Parks

The famous open-air museum of Skansen (see page 45) has a full and varied summer season of outdoor entertainment. This may include anything from a performance by an orchestra to a foreign dance troupe.

Another focal point of enjoyable summer entertainment is Skansen's close neighbor, Tivoli Gröna Lund, on the shore of Djurgården. Crowds flock to the amusement park's open-air stage to be entertained by international performers, which in the past have included such diverse figures as Count Basie and Sven-Bertil Taube.

SPORTS

The Swedes are a very sports-minded people, so it's not surprising that excellent sporting facilities exist throughout the Stockholm region. Top spectator sports are soccer (in the summer) and ice hockey (in the winter). The prestigious sports events, such as the ice hockey championships, are held in the Globe Arena, whose gigantic white dome you may have noticed on the city's south horizon. Reputed to be the largest spherical building anywhere in the world, the Arena can be transformed rapidly from a sports stadium into a theater or a concert hall.

Watersports such as sailing, swimming, and fishing are very popular, as you would expect in a city that virtually floats on water. Swedes of all ages are also fond of jogging and cross-country skiing, and there are many trails for these activities in nearby wooded areas.

A number of recreational facilities are centered in Djurgården, where you can rent a bike, go horseback riding, and enjoy peaceful promenading. Get in touch with the Stockholm Information Service (<www.stockholmtown.com>) for up-to-date information on sports around the city.

Winter is no reason to stay indoors — take a Sunday stroll
on the ice while the sun is still shining.

Swimming. In the Stockholm region there are 200 km (125 miles) of beaches — both sea and lake bathing — including several at Riddarfjärden, near the center of town. Bear in mind that the water hardly ever gets really warm (above 20°C/68°F). If it is too cold for you, there are seven outdoor pools, some with saunas, in the city, and dozens of others in the suburbs, open from May to mid-September. One of the most pleasant pools is Vanadisbadet, near Sveavägen, which has been converted into a beautiful water park with water-slides. The biggest is Eriksdalsbadet, on the south side of the city, which can accommodate 3,000 people.

Fishing. Pollution has been eliminated from Stockholm's waters in the last few years, and it's now possible to fish for salmon in Strömmen, the stream that flows past the Royal Palace. There is good fishing in Lake Mälaren, in the smaller lakes in the city environs, and around the 24,000 islands of the archipelago in the Baltic Sea. A fishing permit is not required in the city, but is elsewhere. For more information call the Anglers Association Stockholm, Tel. (08) 19 78 20, between 10am and 1pm.

Sailing. There is plenty of company for sailing enthusiasts in Stockholm. During the summer months there are numerous boats on Lake Mälaren, in the archipelago, and skimming through the city's waterways. There are at least ten places in the Stockholm area where boats can be rented (again, check with the tourist office) and special harbors for visitors with their own boats. A word of warning, however: If you are planning to sail through the labyrinth of islands that make up the Stockholm archipelago, you must know what you're doing. It's a beautiful experience, but not to be attempted by amateurs.

Canoeing. Sweden is very well-equipped for canoeists. For rental equipment contact Kanotbryggan Adventure Sport, Karlbergs Strand 4, Tel. (08) 83 82 90.

Golf. There are now more than 380 golf courses in Sweden, including one beyond the Arctic Circle where it's possible to play under the light of the midnight sun. In the Stockholm area the following golf courses stand out: Djursholms Golfklubb, Tel. (08) 755 14 77; and Saltsjöbadens Golfklubb, Tel. (08) 717 01 26.

Tennis. You might have some trouble getting a court in the evening and on weekends, but otherwise it should not be too crowded. Two of the very best venues, both with indoor and outdoor courts, are Tennisstadion, Tel. (08) 21 54 54; and the Kungliga Tennishallen, Tel. (08) 459 15 00.

Hiking. The hallowed tradition of allemansrätten, meaning that you can walk just about anywhere you want in Sweden as long as you don't damage anyone else's property, guarantees everyone an equal right to enjoy nature. There are plenty of easy, marked walking trails. The summer trails are indicated by raised or painted stones and all-season trails by crosses. For those in search of more organized itineraries, marked trails start just outside Stockholm. Ambitious hikers can follow a trail called "Upplandsleden" from Järfälla to Uppsala and from Baålsta to Enköping. To the east of Stockholm, the trail called "Roslagsleden" extends 56 km (35 miles) between Danderyd and Domarudden.

Skating. The most popular and most conspicuous outdoor rink is in Kungsträdgården in the center of town. However, many Swedes do prefer long-distance skating along the frozen waterways of Lake Mälaren and the Baltic Sea in winter, when the ice is thick enough. You can rent skates.

In the summer, you can watch the masts of the sailing regattas throughout Stockholm and its archipelago.

Get up close and personal with the animals at Skansen — there are some for petting and even a few for riding!

Skiing. Swedes enjoy skiing, both the downhill and cross-country versions. There are several ski resorts in Stockholm and at Västmanland, north of Lake Mälaren. A particularly fine ski center is at Mora on Lake Siljan. For cross-country skiing you will need a map of the route and suitable clothing.

STOCKHOLM FOR CHILDREN

Children can have a lot of fun in Stockholm, a city with a large number of family activities appealing to both young and old. One major attraction not to be overlooked is the archipelago's countless islets. Many children ask for nothing more than a boat ride and the chance to climb among the rocks or to fish or swim. However, there are numerous other highlights in the city to keep children well occupied.

On all public transport in Stockholm, children under 7 years of age travel free, while children between 7 and 18 pay half price. With a Stockholm Card, which enables free travel on the underground, buses, and local trains, two children under 18 may be included for free when accompanied by an adult who has purchased the card (see page 125).

Aquaria: At this fascinating water museum in Djurgården, children can follow the course of a rain-forest river from the mountains to the open sea, among other attractions (see page 43).

Changing of the Guard: A captivating experience for children of all ages (see page 34).

Gröna Lund: This amusement park, which is only open during the summer months, has rides, a fun-house, and other amusing activities for children (see page 44).

Skansen: This open-air museum's zoo has a section devoted to baby farm animals that children can get close to and pet. There is also an aquarium and a crocodile pond (see page 45).

Tekniskamuseet (Technical Museum): Older children will be fascinated by the exhibits, especially the computers (see page 61).

Vasamuseet (Vasa Museum): Children will enjoy this bit of Swedish history (see page 41).

Leksaksmuseet (Toy Museum): Mariatorget 1C, Tel. (08) 641 61 00. A variety of interesting toys are on display here. Open Tuesday–Friday 10am–4pm, and Saturday and Sunday midday–4pm, and open on Monday in the summer. Entrance 40kr adults and 20kr for children.

Restaurants: Many restaurants have special half-price children's menus. Stockholm also has many fast-food chains.

Calendar of Events

The Swedes may be ultra-modern in their social and sexual attitudes, but they are very traditional when it comes to celebrations. Throughout the year, festivals brighten up the calendar. (For a comprehensive list of public holidays in Sweden, see page 116)

30 April: Walpurgis Night has its roots in Viking times. Huge bonfires blaze across the landscape, saluting the arrival of spring. The university towns are especially exuberant; students hold torchlight parades and toast spring in verse, speeches, and songs.

1 May: May Day is given over to labor groups.

June: On Archipelago Boat Day numerous steamboats make their way over to Vaxholm Island.

6 June: The Swedish National Day is celebrated with flags, parades, and supersonic jets streaking across the sky. There is a ceremony when the King and Royal Family (Queen Silvia in Swedish national costume) present flags to organizations and individuals.

Friday between 19 June and 25 June: On the longest day of the year (Midsummer Eve), colorful maypoles decorated with garlands of birch boughs and wildflowers are raised in village and town squares all over Sweden. After the maypole goes up, everyone joins hands and dances around it to the tunes of country fiddlers. The dancing, along with a fair amount of drinking and merry-making, continues far into the night, which in midsummer is as bright as day. In Stockholm, anyone can join the Midsummer Eve festivities at Skansen.

October: World's largest cross-country race held at Lidingö.

10 December: Nobel Prize Day.

13 December: One of the winter highlights is St. Lucia Day, a beguiling pre-Christmas ceremony. Young girls dressed in long white gowns are crowned with wreaths of lighted candles that symbolize light breaking through the winter darkness. They sing a special Lucia song and serve fresh buns and coffee. If you're in Sweden on this day, you'll see candles in almost every coffee shop and restaurant.

EATING OUT

The best way to describe the Swedish approach to food is "natural." A Swede can become quite lyrical at the thought of färskpotatis, a dish of new potatoes boiled with dill (a commonly used herb in Sweden) and served with a pat of butter. Wild berries and mushrooms are highly prized, especially since food prices have skyrocketed in recent years. Swedish law gives everyone the right, known as alle-mansrätten, to wander through fields and forests to pick these gifts of nature. Even city-dwellers, never too far away from the great outdoors, take the opportunity to gather smul-tron (wild strawberries), blåbär (bilberries, or blueberries), hjortron (Arctic cloudberries), svamp (mushrooms), and lin-gon (wild cranberries).

In Sweden each season has its traditional specialities, and any discussion of eating habits must take these into account. Some regional dishes, such as blood soup and fermented her-ring, may sound less than appetizing, but those visitors with more adventurous palates will want to try at least a few of those foods that the calendar and time-honored custom prescribe.

Restaurants

Stockholm offers a great variety of dining establishments. During recent years pizzerias, hamburger chains, and Chinese restaurants have spread widely, while many other restaurants specialize in international cuisine. There is also, of course, a Hard Rock Café at Sveavägen 75, <www.hardrock-se.com>. The real problem nowadays is finding genuine, old-fashioned Swedish food.

Look for restaurants that serve husmanskost — traditional, everyday Swedish dishes. A few you might try: *Janssons fres-telse* (Jansson's Temptation), a delicious casserole of potatoes, sprats, onion, and cream; *Kåldolmar*, stuffed cabbage rolls; *pytt i panna*, finely diced meat, onions, and potatoes together; *kalops*, beef stew; *dillkött*, lamb or veal in dill sauce; *köttbullar*, the famous Swedish meatballs; *bruna bönor*, baked brown beans in a molasses sauce; *strömmingsflundror*, a fried boned herring; and on Thursdays, join almost the entire local populace in eating *ärter med fläsk*, yellow pea soup with pork, followed by *pannkakor med sylt*, pancakes with jam.

The *smörgåsbord* can be hard to find sometimes, except on Sunday afternoons and during the Christmas season. Every day the elegant Operakällaren (the Opera Restaurant) in Stockholm has a luncheon smörgåsbord reputed to be the best in the world. Otherwise, ask the receptionist at your hotel for advice on this subject.

Eating out in Stockholm is not cheap, but prices at the top-flight restaurants are generally in line with comparable establishments in other European cities. Having pre-dinner cocktails in a restaurant or bar, on the other hand, can make a real dent in your budget; better to have wine or beer with your meal. There are many inexpensive self-service cafeterias throughout the city, and most restaurants have small portions for children at half price. Also look for the *Dagens rätt* (dish of the day), as this is usually a good bet.

Lunch tends to be served around midday, and dinner from 6pm. A service charge is normally added to the restaurant bill, though the waiter or waitress may also hope for a small extra tip — maybe 10% if you are satisfied with the service.

Breakfast and Bread

A Swedish breakfast (*frukost*) usually consists of a cup of coffee or tea with rolls, butter, and marmalade, and sometimes cheese. A much more substantial breakfast with eggs, bacon, or ham will certainly be available at your hotel.

An authentic Swedish smörgåsbord is not as easy to find as you might think, but the reward is worth the hunt!

Coffee — which is excellent in Sweden — is consumed in great quantities at all times of the day and night, and forms a recognized part of Swedish social life. The Swedes (even adults) also drink a lot of milk with their meals. In addition, yogurt and other kinds of fermented milk are popular.

Until recently, many people complained about the Swedish bread (which has molasses in it) as being too sweet. As a result, unsweetened bread is being made and widely sold. Be sure to try *knäckebröd* (crisp rye bread), which comes in a wide selection and is something worth taking back home, along with some cheese: there are, so it is claimed, more than 200 different cheeses to choose from. Look for *vasterbottenost*, *herrgardsost*, and *sveciaost* — these are typical hard, well-aged cheeses.

Spring and Summer Specialities

As the name implies, *fettisdagsbullar* or *semlor* (Shrove Tuesday buns) are associated with Lent, but they are now so popular that they appear on the market right after Christmas. The baked buns are split, filled with an almond paste and whipped cream, and served in a deep dish with hot milk, sugar, and cinnamon. The arrival of spring is traditionally celebrated with another calorie-packed treat, *våfflor* (crisp waffles served with jam and whipped cream), as well as three salmon delicacies — *gravad lax*, pickled salmon in dill served with mustard sauce, *färskrökt lax*, smoked salmon, and *kokt lax*, or boiled salmon.

Summertime means almost 24-hour daylight in Sweden. It's a season when people in this northern climate can luxuriate in fruit and vegetables that have been grown locally under the midnight sun, instead of the expensive imported produce available during much of the year. Look for

Friendly crowds congregate at Café Opera, one of Stockholm's most famous restaurants and nightclubs.

västkustsallad, a delicious seafood salad that also contains tomatoes and mushrooms.

A delightful custom not to be missed by anyone visiting Sweden in August is the *kräftor* (crayfish) party. This is when Swedes abandon all rules of table etiquette as they attack mounds of small lobster-like creatures gleaming bright red in the light from gay paper lanterns strung above the tables. *Kryddost* (cheese spiced with caraway), buttered toast, and fresh berries complete the traditional menu. The mood can become quite festive as liberal amounts of aquavit are usually downed on this occasion. This highly potent drink accompanies another seasonal speciality, *surströmming* (salted and fermented Baltic herring). Indeed, many people can't get this fish past their nose without the aid of a dram or two of aquavit. The smell, to put it mildly, is staggering. Even so, some Swedes, particularly those from the northern part of the country, consider the dish a great delicacy.

Autumn and Winter Fare

Although southern Sweden is the best place to celebrate St. Martin's Day, you can usually find restaurants that observe the tradition in Stockholm as well. The star of this November event is *stekt gås* (roast goose), but the first course and dessert probably deserve the most attention. You begin the meal with a highly spiced *svartsoppa* (blood soup) and finish with *spettekaka*, a lace-like pyramid cake baked on a spit: it melts in your mouth.

The Christmas season gets off to an early, charming start in Sweden on 13 December — one of the darkest and shortest days of the year — when Lucia makes her early morning appearance in many homes and even in public places. Dressed in a long white robe, with a crown of lighted candles on her head, the Queen of Light awakens the sleeping house by singing the special Lucia song and serving saffron buns, ginger snaps, and coffee.

Christmas is preceded by weeks of preparation in the kitchen. Though no longer the feast it once was, the Yuletide smörgåsbord (*julbord*) still retains its essential ingredients.

Systembolaget

Teetotaller organizations are a powerful factor in Swedish politics and this has led to very high taxes on alcoholic beverages, especially hard liquor, as a means of trying to discourage drinking. Also, with the exception of a very weak beer that can be bought in grocery stores or supermarkets, alcoholic beverages are sold only in the shops of the Systembolaget, the state-owned liquor monopoly.

These Systembolaget shops do stock a vast range of recognized brands of whisky, vodka, gin, and so forth, but wine is by far the best value for your money. Popular table wines (which are French, Italian, Spanish, and Greek) are shipped to Sweden in huge tankers and bottled here. The quality is good, the selection is wide, and the prices are relatively moderate. This is all part of the Systembolaget campaign, involving the promotion of wine drinking — but in moderate quantities, of course — while simultaneously conducting a propaganda campaign against the evils of consuming hard liquor.

Systembolaget stores are recognizable by a green-and-yellow rectangular sign and are usually open Monday–Friday 9am–6pm and Saturday to 4pm and closed Sunday, although these hours can vary slightly from store to store. There can be self-service or over-the-counter service; only some take credit cards and you have to be 20 years of age to purchase the alcohol.

Restaurants also often make a special feature of the smörgåsbord around the holidays.

However, the smörgåsbord is only part of the Swedish holiday menu. Other dishes are *lutfisk* (cod that has been dried and cured in lye), *risgrynsgröt* (rice porridge that contains one almond destined to be found by the person to be wed in the coming year), and some *skinka* (ham). This time of year also brings forth all kinds of delicious breads and pastries.

The Smörgåsbord

Bounded by the sea and with some 96,000 lakes dotting its countryside, Sweden has an abundant supply of fish, which naturally plays an important role in the country's diet. In the old days fish was often dried, smoked, cured, or fermented to preserve it for the winter. Even today, in the age of the deep freeze, these methods are still among some of the favorite ways of preparing herring and other treasures from the sea. The herring buffet, or *sillbord*, the predecessor of the smörgåsbord, is still the basis of Sweden's most famous culinary attraction.

The smörgåsbord table (or groaning board, if you will) can consist of as many as 100 different dishes. It should not be tackled haphazardly. The first thing to remember is not to overload your plate — you can go back for more as many times as you wish.

Even more important is the order in which you eat. Start off by sampling the innumerable herring dishes, taken with boiled potatoes and bread and butter. Then move on to other seafood, like smoked or boiled salmon, smoked eel, Swedish caviar, and shrimp. Next come the delightful egg dishes, cold meats (try the smoked reindeer), and salads. The small warm dishes are next — meatballs, fried sausages, and omelets — and finally (if you still have room), you finish with cheese and fruit.

Alcoholic Beverages

The Swedish national drink is aquavit, also called snaps, which is distilled from potatoes or grain and flavored with herbs and spices, and there are many varieties. Aquavit should always be consumed with food, especially herring; it should be ice-cold and served up in small glasses, consumed straight in a grand gulp or two and washed down with a beer or mineral water. It is closely linked to the word *skål*, the universally recognized Scandinavian toast, delivered as you look straight into the eyes of your drinking companion. When you see a bottle with the word LINE on it, you'll know it's special stuff. In the old days, barrels of aquavit went with the sailors and they swore that it tasted better after having returned from a voyage that had crossed the equator. These days the custom is continued. Barrels are specially sent to cross the line, and when they return the liquor is bottled and the details of the voyage are detailed on the back of the label, and can be read through the bottle.

Among other Swedish alcoholic specialities are *glögg*, a hot, spiced wine that appears during the Christmas season, and *punsch* (punch), which is usually served after dinner,

There are many nice small outdoor cafés to choose from in the Old Town.

well-chilled, with coffee. It can also be drunk hot with the traditional Swedish Thursday dinner of yellow pea soup and pancakes.

To Help You Order ...

beer	öl	meat	kött
bread	bröd	menu	matsedeln
butter	smör	milk	mjölk
cheese	ost	mineral water	mineralvatten
coffee	kaffe	potatoes	potatis
cream	grädde	sandwich	smörgås
dessert	efterrätt	soup	soppa
fish	fisk	sugar	socker
fruit	frukt	tea	te
ice cream	glass	wine	vin

... and Read the Menu

biff	beef steak	matjessill	pickled herring
böckling	smoked herring	musslor	mussels, clams
fläskkotlett	pork chop	nyponsoppa	rose-hip soup
fromage	mousse	oxstek	roast beef
gädda	pike	paj	pie
jordgubbar	strawberries	räkor	shrimps
kalv	veal	rensadel	saddle of reindeer
kasseler	smoked pork loin		
korv	sausage	rödspätta	plaice
krabba	crab	rotmos	mashed turnips
krusbär	gooseberries	sillbullar	herring rissoles
kyckling	chicken	skaldjur	shellfish
lammstek	roast lamb	skinka	ham
lax	salmon	sparris	asparagus
lever	liver	spenat	spinach
lök	onion	vitkål	white cabbage

HANDY TRAVEL TIPS

An A–Z Summary of Practical Information

A

ACCOMMODATIONS (*hotell*; *logi*) (See also CAMPING, YOUTH HOSTELS, and the list of Recommended Hotels starting on page 128) Hotels in Stockholm, as elsewhere in Sweden, have a well-deserved reputation for cleanliness, facilities, good service and, unfortunately, rather small rooms, regardless of their price category. In reality, however, the vast majority of the hotels are what would be considered, if there were a standardized rating system, in the three- or four-star class, and thus not inexpensive. It is advisable to book accommodations in advance; to assist with this either ask for the informative brochure *Hotels in Sweden* at the Swedish tourist office in your country or check it out on the Internet at <www.hotelsinsweden. net>. This web site also has links to many of the hotel groups and to other sites of interest to travelers to Sweden. Also, the Stockholm Information Service publishes a very informative booklet called *Hotels and Youth Hostels in Stockholm*.

The Stockholm Package is worth consideration. From 455Sek per person, in 2000, you could choose from 55 hotels in a range of prices and the package included accommodations, breakfast, and the Stockholm Card (see page 125). The Stockholm Package could be booked all days of the week between 1 June and 31 August, and on weekends and holidays the rest of the year.

Some hotel chains operate plans of their own, or in conjunction with other groups, enabling you to get certain discounts. For example, Sweden Hotels, Tel. (08) 701 79 00; <www.swedenhotels.se>, offer the *Check In* plan allowing the advance purchase of a booklet of 12 vouchers, or the *SCAN* + plan, in conjunction with other groups, allowing a discount at 200 hotels in Scandinavia.

Hotellcentralen, Centralstationen (Central Station), SE-111 20, Tel. (08) 789 24 56; fax (08) 791 86 66; e-mail <hotels@ stoinfo.se>, operated by the Stockholm Information Service, offers free advance booking of hotels, direct booking of hotels and youth hostels, booking of special City and Weekend Packages and other general tourist information. Between May and September it opens daily from 7am–9pm and from October to April it opens daily from 9am–6pm. It is possible, however, that hours may change on public holidays. There is an unmanned, automatic hotel reservation system at Arlanda airport.

Bed & Breakfast accommodations in Stockholm can be arranged by the following: **Bed & Breakfast Agency,** Tel. (08) 643 80 28; fax (08) 643 80 78; **Bed and Breakfast Center**, Tel. (08) 730 00 03; fax (08) 730 52 14 or **Bed and Breakfast Service**, Tel. (08) 700 62 72; (08); fax (08) 696 00 48.

AIRPORT (*flygplat*)

All flights to Stockholm are handled by Arlanda airport, located 41 km (26 miles) from the city. The airport has four terminals, two — numbers 5 and 2 — for international flights, and two — numbers 3 and 4 — for domestic flights. Inter-terminal buses transfer passengers between the terminals. The airport telephone number is (08) 797 60 00.

The fastest way to and from Stockholm's Centralstationen (Central Station) and Arlanda airport, just 20 minutes' distance, is on the Arlanda Express train, Tel. (08) 595 114 40; fax (08) 595 114 50; web site <www.arlandaexpress.com>. These run every 15 minutes between 5am and midnight and the fare is 120kr each way. Beware, though, there is a 30kr surcharge if you wait to purchase the ticket on the train. During the summer of 2000 a two-for-the-price-of-one ticket was available — a real bargain.

Airport buses *Flygbussarna*, Tel. (08) 686 10 00; fax (08) 686 37 97, depart from the City terminal, Klarabergsviadukten, every 10 minutes and take approximately 35 minutes. The fare is 60kr each way.

Taxis are very expensive, but insist on the fixed rate that varies between 350–425kr.

B

BICYCLE RENTAL (*cykel*)

You can rent a bicycle at Cykel & Mopeduthyrning, Strandvägen, kajplats 24, Tel. (08) 660 79 59, where the typical cost is 150kr per day. Note that heavy traffic can make bicycling in Stockholm difficult, except in a few places like Djurgården, the big island park.

BUDGETING FOR YOUR TRIP

The following are some prices in Swedish kronor (kr) to help you plan your travelling budget. However, remember that all these prices must be regarded as approximate and cannot account for inflation.

Car rental. Prices vary considerably. All quotes are for unlimited mileage. A small car (e.g., Ford Escort) for three days costs 1,615kr; for the week 2,655kr. A larger car (e.g., Saab 9-5) for three days is 2,425kr; for the week 3,985kr.

Guides. These are not cheap; in 2000 the minimum cost was 1,300kr for up to three hours.

Hotels. Prices at the lower end can be difficult to find, but prices at the top end may rise considerably above 2,000kr. (See also ACCOMMODATIONS and the list of Recommended Hotels starting on page 128)

Meals and drinks. Continental breakfast in a restaurant/café costs 50kr; lunch 80–100kr; dinner at a medium-priced restaurant (not including drinks) 250kr per head. Coffee or soft drinks cost 20kr; a bottle of wine 150kr minimum and often much more; spirits (4cl) 75kr, except aquavit (4cl) 50kr. Look for the sign *Dagens rätt* (dish of the day): salad, a main course, and coffee, which is usually a good value.

Alcohol. This is especially expensive, and any alcohol over 3.5% has to be purchased at Systembolaget, a state-run chain of stores. (See page 100)

Stockholm

Museums. The cost is usually between 40–80kr, although some are free.

Gas. In the summer of 2000 this approached 10kr per litre. There are petrol stations with automatic 24-hour pumps that take 100kr notes.

Public transport. A single ticket for the bus and subway (*tunnelbana*) is 16kr.

Stockholm Card (Stockholmskort). Its validity is for one, two, or three days and costs 220kr and 60kr, 380kr and 120kr and 540kr and 180kr, for adults and children, respectively. (See TOURIST INFORMATION, page 125)

Taxis. These are, price wise, entirely unregulated and the fare for the same ride can vary enormously. Reliable companies are Taxi Kurir, Tel. (08) 30 00 00; and Taxi Stockholm, Tel. (08) 15 00 00.

CAMPING

The closest camping ground is Östermalms City Camping, Fiskartorpsvägen 2, SE-114 33, Tel. (08) 10 29 03; fax (08) 21 44 12. It is 1.5 km (about a mile) from the city center and open late June to late August. For a complete list of local sites request the booklet *CAMPING STOCKHOLM The Official Tourist Guide to Camping in Stockholm*. This is published by the Stockholm Information Service, and also gives other useful information and requirements for camping in Stockholm.

Cabins: These are available for rent throughout the archipelago. For more information contact Hotellcentralen (see ACCOMMODATIONS above) or The Excursion Shop, Tel. (08) 789 24 56; fax (08) 789 24 91; e-mail <info@stoinfo.se>.

CAR RENTAL (*biluthyrning*) (See also DRIVING IN SWEDEN and BUDGETING FOR YOUR TRIP)

In reality, visitors to Stockholm, and the numerous attractions in its immediate vicinity, will find that having a car is more of a hindrance than an assistance. The public transport system is superb and the numerous boats that ply the waters of the archipelago and Lake Mälaren are an attraction in their own right. Besides that, car rental, like gas, is not inexpensive and the penalties for drunk driving and other restrictions are severe.

However, notwithstanding that, if you are planning to tour around the country, or just feel you want a car, then renting a car before you go can avoid any uncertainties. Auto europe, Tel. 1 800 223 5555; fax (207) 842-2222; web site <www.autoeurope.com>, is the largest organization operating in North America and often offers the best rates available.

If you decide to rent once you are in Stockholm, then you can contact Avis, Tel. 020 78 82 00; Budget, Tel. (08) 21 06 50; Europcar, Tel. 020 78 77 87; or Hertz, Tel. 020 21 12 11. These are toll free numbers and can only be dialed within Sweden.

The legal minimum driving age in Sweden is 18, but to rent a car you usually need to have held a license for three years so, in practice, the minimum age is 21. You'll need your driver's license and passport. Most companies require a deposit, but this is waived if you present an accepted credit card.

CLIMATE and CLOTHING

Climate. Most of Sweden has a continental climate, with a medium to large temperature difference between summer and winter. In summer temperatures do rise above 20°C (70°F). Summer is, of course, the prime season to visit Stockholm. In midsummer, daylight lasts up to 19 hours, with lots of sunshine — and lots of other visitors. In spring, which is particularly lovely in the lake district and outlying regions, and autumn, with bright colors and clear nights, you'll have Sweden to yourself. Winter is tempting for sports enthusiasts and Christmas in Sweden can be an unforgettable experience.

The following chart will give you an idea of the average daily maximum and minimum temperatures, and average number of rainy days each month in Stockholm.

Stockholm

	J	F	M	A	M	J	J	A	S	O	N	D
Max °F	31	31	37	45	57	65	70	66	58	48	38	33
Min	23	22	26	32	41	49	55	53	46	39	31	26
Max °C	-1	-1	3	7	14	18	21	19	14	9	3	1
Min	-5	-6	-3	0	5	9	13	12	8	4	-1	-3
Days of rainfall	10	7	6	7	7	8	9	10	9	9	10	11

Clothing: Although the weather is usually very pleasant during the day in the short summer months, it cools enough at night to make a sweater or light jacket necessary. Beware, also, the weather can be unpredictable, so pack a light waterproof coat. In the spring and fall heavier clothing will be required, while in winter warm boots and heavy jackets are necessary. Appropriate shoes are also needed as visiting the Old Town and other parts of Stockholm require much walking.

Stockholmers no longer dress up as they used to, and even at the theater, concert, or opera, smart casual clothes are the rule. There are a few late-opening restaurants that require (or expect) guests to wear a tie and jacket.

COMPLAINTS

The Swedish sense of fair play makes complaining a rare event, and complaints themselves often unnecessary. In a restaurant or hotel, a quiet word with the manager is usually enough. Serious complaints about hotels or other major services should be directed to the Stockholm Information Service tourist offices or to the appropriate travel authority.

CRIME (See also EMERGENCIES and POLICE)

Sweden is one of the safest countries in the world. Nevertheless, like other cities, Stockholm has kept up with the times, which means that crime has increased. And although you are not likely to get mugged, there were warnings in the hotels in 2000 advising visitors not to leave bags unattended in the breakfast rooms and restaurants. This, obviously, is good policy anywhere and it is also good policy to check your valuables — including passport and airline tickets — into the hotel safe. Another sensible precaution is to take photocopies of passports and airline tickets and keep them separate from the originals. In instances where the originals are stolen, lost, or damaged this will save an enormous amount of time and hassle. Certain parts of the city, such as parks like Humlegården, can be a bit dangerous — or very unpleasant — late at night.

Any loss or theft should be reported at once to the nearest police station, if only for insurance purposes; your insurance company will need to see a copy of the police report.

CUSTOMS AND ENTRY FORMALITIES (*tull*)

Visitors from EU countries need only an identity card to enter Sweden. Citizens of most other countries must be in possession of a valid passport, while South African citizens need a visa. Contact the Embassy of Sweden, 1166 Park Street, P.O. Box 13477, Hatfield 0028, South Africa; Tel. (27) 12 4266400; fax (27) 12 4266464. European and North American residents are not subject to any health requirements. In case of doubt, check with Swedish representatives in your own country before departure.

Duty-free allowance. As Sweden is part of the European Union, free exchange of non-duty-free goods for personal use is permitted between Sweden and other EU countries. Due to the high prices of alcohol and tobacco visitors might consider bringing in some of their own. If so, each person over 20 is allowed 1 litre of liquor (over 22% by volume) and those over 15 may carry with them 300 cigarettes if living in the EU and 400 if living outside the EU.

Currency restrictions. There is no restriction on the amount of foreign or local currency you may bring into or take out of the country as a tourist (provided it is declared upon entry).

Stockholm

DRIVING in SWEDEN (See also Car Rental)

Drive on the right, pass on the left. Traffic on main roads (and very often main streets in town) has the right-of-way. Maximum speed limits are indicated by signs on all roads. Traffic on roundabouts usually has priority, but in other situations traffic from the right has right-of-way. You must also give way to anyone in a crosswalk and to any cyclist who is crossing a cycle track. It is obligatory to use seat belts, including back-seat passengers. Children under seven should be secured in the back seat with a harness or in a child seat.

Drinking and driving is a very serious offense. The police are free to stop motorists and breathalize them whenever they want to. You can be fined or even sent to jail if your alcohol level exceeds 0.2 per mille.

If you have serious car trouble, you can either contact the police or call Larmtjänst (which is a 24-hour breakdown service), a company owned by the Swedish insurance companies. Their toll free number from anywhere in Sweden: (020) 22 00 00.

ELECTRICITY

The supply for electric appliances in Sweden is 220 volt, 50 Hz AC, and requires standard two-pin, round continental plugs. Visitors should bring their own adapters.

EMBASSIES/CONSULATES

The embassies, with consulate sections, are generally open Monday–Friday from 8am–4pm, but there is usually a 24-hour telephone service. New Zealand does not have an embassy in Sweden.

Australia: Embassy: Sergels Torg 12, Box 7003, SE-103 86, Stockholm; Tel. (08) 613 29 00; fax (08) 24 74 14; e-mail <info@austemb.se>.

Canada: Embassy: Tegelbacken 4, Box 16129, SE-103 23, Stockholm; Tel. (08) 453 30 00; fax (08) 24 24 91; web site <www. canadaemb.se>.

Republic of Ireland: Embassy: Östermalmsgatan 97, Box 10326, ES-100 55, Stockholm; Tel. (08) 661 80 05; fax (08) 660 13 53.

South Africa: Embassy: Linnégatan 76, SE-115 23, Stockholm; Tel. (08) 24 39 50; fax (08) 660 71 36.

UK: Embassy: Skarpögatan 6-8, Box 27819, SE-115 93 Stockholm; Tel. (08) 671 90 00; fax (08) 662 99 89; web site <www.britishembassy.com>.

USA: Embassy: Dag Hammarskjölds väg 31, SE-115 89, Stockholm; Tel. (08) 783 53 00; fax (08) 660 58 79; web site <www.usemb.se>.

EMERGENCIES (See also POLICE and MEDICAL CARE)
The general emergency telephone number in Sweden is 112. This number covers the ambulance, rescue service, fire department, police, air/sea and mountain rescue services, the poison hot line and on-call doctors. It can be dialed free (no coins needed) from any telephone. English is usually understood.

G

GAY and LESBIAN TRAVELERS
Sweden is one of the world's most progressive countries when it comes to gay rights. Since 1988 government legislation has granted gay relationships the same status as heterosexual marriages and the state has given financial support to gay organizations. Information and advice can be obtained from the Swedish Federation for Lesbian and Gay Rights: R.S.F.L. (Riksförbundet för Sexuellt Likaberätti-gade), Stockholms Gay-hus, Sveavägen 57. (Postal address: Förbundskansli, Box 350, S-101-26 Stockholm); Tel. (08) 736 02 13.

GETTING TO STOCKHOLM

Air Travel
From the USA & Canada: SAS (Scandinavian Airlines System), Tel. 1 800 221 2350; web site <www.flysas.com>, operates daily flights to Stockholm from Newark and Chicago. ICELANDAIR, Tel. 1 800 223 5500; web site <www.icelandair.com>, has flights to and from

Stockholm

Stockholm, with a change of flight in Reykjavik (offering a great opportunity for a stopover in Iceland), from Baltimore/Washington, Boston, Halifax, Nova Scotia, New York City, and Orlando, Florida.

From Europe: There are flights from many destinations that are direct to Stockholm.

From Australia and New Zealand: There are no direct flights from these countries. Depending upon the city of destination, Quantas, the Australian national airline, operates in conjunction with other airlines, flights to Stockholm that necessitate two, sometimes three, changes, usually in the Far East and then Europe. Air New Zealand operates flights from Auckland to London and then from London on BA to Stockholm.

From South Africa: South African Airlines does not operate flights to Stockholm.

Rail Travel

Stockholm, on the eastern coast of Sweden, is easily accessible by rail from Copenhagen, Denmark, and Oslo, Norway, but connections to Helsinki, Finland, are best made by way of a direct ferry, or a ferry to Turku, Finland, and then by train.

Rail Passes. Rail Europe; Tel. 1 888 382 7245; web site <www.raileurope.com>, offers a whole variety of rail passes for non-European citizens, that must be purchased before leaving home, and can be used in Sweden alone or in Sweden and other countries. The Inter-Rail Card, which can be purchased in Europe, is valid for one month's unlimited second-class travel in Europe for young people under 26, for whom there are also discount fares.

By Sea

You can travel with or without your car from the UK ports of Harwich or Newcastle to Gothenburg (Göteborg). Then, by car, the E20 (formerly E3) is the most direct route from Gothenburg to Stockholm.

GUIDES AND TOURS (*guide*)

The Stockholm Information Service operates a private Guide & Group Booking service, Tel. (08) 789 24 96; fax 789 24 45, and books transportation and authorized guides for individuals and groups. Currently 28 languages are catered to, and the minimum fee is 1,300kr for up to 3 hours. Taxi Guides — specially trained taxi drivers who serve as guides and are available in 11 languages — are available for 480kr for the first hour and 420kr for each subsequent hour for four people.

H

HEALTH & MEDICAL CARE

Medical Care (See also EMERGENCIES)

No vaccinations are needed for entry to Sweden. Citizens of other EU countries, providing they are in possession of a valid E-111 form, are treated free in Sweden. Citizens of non-EU countries should ensure they have adequate travel/health insurance before leaving home.

If you fall ill, have an accident, or are in need of a doctor, call the 24-hour medical advice hot line, Tel. (08) 463 91 00, or ask someone such as your hotel receptionist to call a doctor for you. Make sure the doctor is affiliated with Försäktringskassan (Swedish National Health Service). If you are able, go to a hospital's emergency and casualty reception (akutmottagning); take your passport with you for identification. Any prescriptions need to be taken to a chemist (*apoteket*). A free health care information service can be reached at Tel. (08) 644 92 00.

Dental treatment. A dental surgery is called *tandläkare* in Swedish. For emergency dental treatment go to the clinic called Akuttandvården at St. Eriks Sjukhus, Fleminggatan 22, SE-112 82 Stockholm; Tel. (08) 654 11 17, open daily 8am–8pm. No appointments are accepted. After 7pm only emergency cases such as accidents, bleeding, etc. are accepted. After 9pm call Tel. (08) 64492 00 for more information.

Chemists/pharmacies (apoteket) stock over-the-counter products like cough-medicine and aspirin and also supply prescriptions. A 24-hour pharmacy service is offered by C.W. Scheele at Klarabergsgatan 64 near the Centralstationen (Central Station); Tel. (08) 454 81 30; fax (08) 791 88 77. Nevertheless, it is a good idea to bring along an adequate supply of any prescribed medication from home. Call toll free, Tel. 020 66 77 66, for pharmacy medication information when in Sweden.

HOLIDAYS (*helgdag*)

Banks, offices, and shops close on public holidays in Sweden, as do most restaurants, museums, food shops, and tourist attractions. Note that many establishments also close early on the day before a holiday — some may even close for the entire day beforehand. On Christmas Eve virtually everything is closed.

1 January	Nyårsdagen	New Year's Day
6 January	Trettondagen	Twelfth Day
1 May	Första Maj	May Day
Sat between 20 and 26 June	Midsommardagen	Midsummer Day
Sat between 31 Oct and 6 Nov	Allhelgonadagen	All Saints' Day
24 December	Julafton	Christmas Eve
25 December	Juldagen	Christmas Day
26 December	Annandag jul	Boxing Day
Movable Dates		
late March/early April	Långfredagen Påskdagen/ Annandag påsk	Good Friday Easter/ Easter Monday

| May | Kristi himmels färdsdag | Ascension Day |
| | Pingstdagen/ Annandag pingst | Whit Sunday/ Monday |

L

LANGUAGE

English is widely spoken and understood all over Sweden, and no English-speaking person visiting the country will have any trouble at all communicating in English. Children study English at school from the age of nine. German is the next choice of language and is spoken by many, particularly in the tourist industry.

Although Swedish is a pleasant language to hear, you are unlikely to find it easy to pronounce. Remember there are three extra letters in the Swedish alphabet, å, ä, and ö, which appear after the usual 26 letters (something to bear in mind when looking up a name in the telephone book).

Days of the week

Sunday	söndag	Thursday	torsdag
Monday	måndag	Friday	fredag
Tuesday	tisdag	Saturday	lördag
Wednesday	onsdag		

Numbers

noll	0	ett	1
två	2	tre	3
fyra	4	fem	5
sex	6	sju	7
åtta	8	nio	9
tio	10	elva	11
tolv	12	tretton	13
fjorton	14	femton	15

Stockholm

sexton	16	sjutton	17
arton	18	nitton	19
tjugo	20	tjugoett	21
trettio	30	fyrtio	40
femtio	50	sextio	60
sjuttio	70	åttio	80
nittio	90	(ett)hundra	100
hundraett	101	hundratio	110
(ett)tusen	1000		

LAUNDRY AND DRY CLEANING (*tvätt; kemtvätt*)

You can get quick service in the hotels and in certain laundry or dry-cleaning establishments, but prices are high, especially for dry cleaning. If you have a lot of laundry, take it to a self-service launderette (Tvättonmat or Tvättbar); one is located at Västmannagatan 61, Tel. (08) 34 64 80.

LOST PROPERTY (*hittegods*)

The main lost property office (*hittegodsexpedition*) is at the police station at Bergsgatan 39, Tel. (08) 401 07 88, open Monday–Friday from 9am–noon and from 1pm–5pm. Taxi drivers deliver lost articles to this office.

For lost property on the main railways go to the lower ground floor of Centralstationen (Central Station), Tel. (08) 762 25 50.

For articles lost on buses and underground trains, contact the Stockholm Local Traffic Office (SL), Tel. (08) 736 07 80, at the Rådmansgatan T-bana underground station, open Monday–Friday from 11am–4pm (Thursday 5pm–7pm).

M

MEDIA

Radio and television: Sveriges Radio (Radio Sweden) and Sveriges Television (Swedish Broadcasting Corporation) used to have a monopoly on all radio and television programs transmitted in

Sweden. Now, however, there are also privately owned radio stations and television channels. Sveriges Radio broadcasts regular 30 minute programs of news and information in English, which can be heard over most of Sweden on medium wave 1179KHz (254m), and also in the Stockholm area on FM 89.6MHz. Further details are available from Radio Sweden International, SE-105 10 Stockholm, Tel. (08) 784 50 00, or from many hotels. Two of the country's five TV channels, SVT1 and SVT2, are financed through license fees, while the others accept advertisements. In addition to Swedish channels, most hotels now carry English-language satellite channels — from the USA and UK, as well as other international stations.

Newspapers and magazines (*tidning*; *tidskrift*): Sweden's main daily newspapers are *Svenska Dagbladet*, *Dagens Nyheter*, and *Göteborgs Posten* (these are broadsheets), and *Expressen* and *Aftonbladet* (these are tabloids), all in Swedish. *The International Herald Tribune* and English papers, as well as a wide variety of magazines, are sold at the Central Railway Station, airport shops, hotels, tobacco shops, and kiosks in central Stockholm. Additionally, some of the top hotels offer them on a complimentary basis.

The Stockholm Information Service publishes a guide to what is happening around the capital, called *What's On*. This is available free, on a monthly basis, from Sweden House, other tourist outlets, and at your hotel.

MONEY

Currency. Sweden's monetary unit is the krona (crown), plural kronor, that is divided into 100 öre, and abbreviated to kr. Confusingly, Sweden, Denmark, and Norway all use the kronor as their national currency, and to distinguish between them they are abbreviated as SEK, DKK and NOK, respectively. (For currency restrictions, see CUSTOMS AND ENTRY FORMALITIES)

Silver coins: 50 öre, 1 krona and 5 kronor. Copper coins: 50 öre. Golden coins: 10 kronor. Banknotes: 20, 50, 100, 500, and 1,000 kronor.

Stockholm

Banks and currency exchange. Foreign currency can be changed in all commercial and savings banks and the larger hotels and department stores. FOREX, web site <www.forex.se>, has offices at Centralstationen (Central Station), the Arlanda Express Terminal, Arlanda Airport and throughout the city that are open daily and advertise that they offer the best exchange rate and lowest commission.

Credit cards and travelers' checks. Most of the international credit cards are welcome; shops and restaurants usually display signs indicating the ones they accept. Travelers' checks can be cashed at the bank or at your hotel. Credit card cancellation numbers: American Express, (08) 429 54 29; Diners (08) 14 68 78; Mastercard 020 79 13 24; Visa, 020 79 31 46. (The 020 prefix indicates a toll free call.)

ATM machines are to be found at almost every bank in Stockholm.

V.A.T./sales tax. This is called Moms in Sweden, and is 25% on all goods and on most services (12% for accommodations). A 14–18% refund is available to non-E.U. residents on products valued at more than 200kr. Moms will be refunded in cash at any point of departure to visitors who have made purchases in shops displaying the blue-and-yellow "Tax-Free Shopping" sticker. You should present your passport at the time of purchase. Later, simply hand over the tax-free shopping check provided by the shop (be sure to fill out the back), at the tax-free service counter in ports, airports, and aboard ships. This refund is available only for a limited period after purchase, and is only open to those who are not Scandinavian residents.

 O

OPEN HOURS

Shops and department stores are usually open weekdays from 9 or 10am to 6pm, Saturdays until 1 or 4pm. Some of the bigger department stores stay open later on weekdays and are open on Sunday afternoons. Food shops have the same hours, but some supermarkets in major underground (subway) stations keep later hours and also open on Sunday afternoons. Certain food shops, *närbutiker*, are open every day of the year from either 7am to 11pm, or 10am to 10pm.

Post offices are generally open Monday–Friday from 9:30am–6pm and Saturday from 10am–1pm. The post office at Centralstationen (Central Station) is open Monday–Friday 7am–10pm and Saturday and Sunday 10am–7pm.

Banks are generally open Monday–Friday from 9:30am–3pm, with some in central Stockholm opening from 9am–5:30pm. Companies like FOREX, an exchange bureau, keep longer hours.

Museums are usually open from 10 or 11am to 4pm. (See also the list of Museums starting on page 52)

Chemists/pharmacies are generally open during normal shopping hours; a number stay open on duty at night and on Sundays. (See MEDICAL CARE)

POLICE (*polis*)

The Stockholm police patrol cars are marked "Polis." Members of the force are invariably courteous and helpful to tourists, and all of them speak some English, so don't hesitate to ask them questions or directions. A police station is located in the Centralstationen (Central Station), Bryggargatan 19, Tel. (08) 401 0000. The emergency police number (also fire, ambulance, etc.) is 112; no money is required from a pay phone.

There are meter maids, dressed in light-blue uniforms, that check the time limits on the parking of cars and issue parking tickets for violations of the restrictions (they do a thorough job). On the motorways and roads the police often carry out routine spot-checks.

POST OFFICES (*postkontor*)

The main post office is at Drottninggatan 53, and opens Monday–Friday 8:30am–6:30pm and Saturday 10am–2pm. The post office at Centralstationen (Central Station), Tel. (08) 781 20 41, opens Monday–Friday 7am–10pm and Saturday and Sunday 10am–7pm. The post office at Arlanda Airport, Terminal 5 (J3), Tel. (08) 593 616 56, opens Monday–Friday 8:30am–6pm.

To receive your mail general delivery (*poste restante*) have it sent to the Central Post Office, Stockholm 1.

PUBLIC TRANSPORTATION

Subway, Bus and Local Trains. Stockholms Lokaltrafik (SL) operates an extremely impressive and efficient bus, subway, and commuter railway system that make it easy to get around the city and its environs from about 5am (a little later on Sundays) to 1am. The subway (*tunnelbana*) has over 100 stations that are indicated by a blue "T" and very creatively decorated, making them an attraction in their own right. There are maps for the underground in the station and on the train, and it is easy to get around on.

Taxis. You can flag taxis down anywhere in Stockholm, find them at stands marked "Taxi," or call them by telephone.

Trains (*tåg*). Swedish State Railway (Statens Järnvägar or S.J.), web site <www.sj.se> operates an extensive network of routes, with trains leaving Stockholm for most big towns every hour or two. The new X2000 high-speed trains which can reach speeds of up to 200 km/h (124 mph) drastically cut the traveling times between Stockholm and other cities within the country.

Boat excursions. Stockholm and its environs are made-to-order for boat excursions. Sightseeing boats cruise under the city's bridges, steamers serve the islands of the archipelago in the Baltic and ply the waters of Lake Mälaren. Full details are available at Sweden House.

R

RELIGION

About 95% of Sweden's native-born population are Lutheran Evangelical, the state-established church. Roman Catholics are estimated at about 60,000 and those of Jewish and other faiths are also represented. Non-Lutheran services are held in the following churches (services are on Sunday at 11am unless otherwise noted):

Anglican: St. Peter and St. Sigfrid, Strandvägen 76, Tel. (08) 663 82 48; in English.

Catholic: St. Eugenia, Kungsträdgärdsgatan 12, Tel. (08) 679 57 70; Sunday at 6pm in English.

Ecumenical International Church: St. Jacobs, Västra Trädgärdsgatan 2, Tel. (08) 723 30 00; Sunday at midday.

Evangelical International Fellowship: Immanuel Church, Kungstensgatan 17, Tel. (08) 674 13 07.

Jewish: Judiska församlingen, Wahrendorffsgatan 3, Tel. (08) 679 29 00.

T

TELEPHONE (*Telefon*).

The country code for Sweden is 46.

The city code for Stockholm is 08; the leading 0, though, is only used for internal calls and is dropped when making an international call to Sweden. Any number beginning with 020 indicates a toll free call.

Predominantly, these days, phone booths take prepaid, disposable telephone cards that can be purchased at a minimum rate of 35kr from Telia shops, Pressbyrån, and other kiosks. There are some booths, identified by a "CCC" sign, that accept credit cards.

Remember, calling home — or anywhere else — from your hotel room is always prohibitively expensive unless, that is, you are using a calling card, or some other similar system, from your local long distance supplier. In which case, find out from that supplier the free connection number applicable to the countries (they are different for each country) you are traveling to before you leave, as these numbers are not always easily available once there. Although dialing these numbers from public telephone booths is nominally toll free, this is not as simple as it seems. It is not possible to connect from coin operated booths without using a prepaid card, against which a small charge is made, to connect to the system before you can actually make a toll free call. For those likely to make such calls, the answer is to purchase a 35kr card upon arrival in Stockholm.

The country code for the USA and Canada is 1, Great Britain 44, Australia 61, New Zealand 64, the Republic of Ireland 353 and South Africa 27.

TIME ZONES

Sweden follows Central European Time (GMT + 1). In summer, the Swedes put their clocks ahead one hour. The following chart shows times across the world in summer:

New York	London	Paris	**Stockholm**	Sydney	Auckland
6am	11am	noon	**noon**	8pm	10pm

TIPPING

Service charges are included in hotel and restaurant bills. Gratuities for waiters, hotel maids, tourist guides, and many others in the tourist-related industries are purely optional. Obviously, a little extra is appreciated for special services rendered, but it isn't expected. In some areas, however, the habit may be more ingrained:

Cloakroom attendant	charges posted or 5kr
Hairdresser/Barber	optional
Hotel porter, per bag	10kr
Taxi driver	tip included in bill
Waiter/Waitress	up to 10% of bill if satisfied

TOILETS (*toalett*)

Public facilities are located in some underground (subway) stations, department stores, and some of the bigger streets, squares, and parks. They are often labelled with symbols for men and women, or marked WC, Damer/Herrar (Ladies/Gentlemen) or simply D/H. Some have slots for coins or an attendant to give towels and soap. The usual charge is 5kr.

TOURIST INFORMATION

In Stockholm the main place to go is the Tourist Center at Sweden House (Sverigehuset), Hamngatan 27, Box 7542, SE-103 93 Stockholm; Tel. (08) 789 24 95, fax (08) 789 24 91; web site <www.stoinfo.se>. This is the main tourist office in Stockholm and offers maps, books, and other tourist information. It is also the home of the Sweden Shop *Sverige Shopen* for souvenirs, the FOREX foreign currency exchange office and the Sweden Bookshop that has information about Sweden in foreign languages and is open on weekdays. Here is also the home of The Excursion Shop *Utflyktsbutiken*, Tel. (08) 789 24 95; fax (08) 789 24 91, that sells tickets for excursions, sightseeing, and concerts; and the Guide and Group Reservations office (See GUIDES AND TOURS, page 115)

Hotellcentralen (See ACCOMMODATIONS, Page 105), also provides tourist information.

The Swedish Travel and Tourism Council also has representatives in the following countries:

USA: Tourist Boards of Denmark, Finland, Iceland, Norway, and Finland, P.O. Box 4649, Grand Central Station, New York, NY, 10163-4649; Tel. (212) 885-9700, fax (212) 885-9710; web site <www.visitsweden.com>.

UK: Swedish Travel & Tourism Council, 11 Montagu Place, London W1H 2AL; Tel. (20) 7724-5869; fax (20) 7724 5872; e-mail <info@swetourism.org.uk>.

The Stockholm Card (Stockholmskortet) offers you the chance to see the city at a reasonable price. It offers the holder free entry to about 70 museums, castles, and other attractions, plus free local public transport — including sightseeing boats, free city center street parking, and more. Used to the full, the card represents a considerable bargain, and each adult can purchase up to two cards for children between the ages of 7 to 17. Its validity is for one, two, or three days and costs 220kr and 60kr, 380kr and 120kr and 540kr and 180kr, for adults and children, respectively (in 2001). These cards can be purchased at Sweden House, Hotellcentralen, some train stations, most tourist offices, camping sites, and youth hostels in and around Stockholm. More information about the Stockholm Card can be found on the web site <www.destinationstockholm.se>.

Throughout Sweden tourist offices (*turistbyrå*) are indicated by the international sign (a white "i" on a green background). There are more than 300 non-profit tourist offices around the country. They stock a good selection of brochures and maps (*karta*) of their respective regions, and can provide you with information on sightseeing, excursions, restaurants, hotels, camping, sports, etc.

W

WEB SITES

The Stockholm Information Service maintains the very wide-ranging and informative site <www.stockholmtown.com>, which can be translated into English, Spanish, and German. The site <www.destinationstockholm.se>, is all about the Stockholm card and if you hit the English flag next to *stockholms-kortet* it brings up a page with numerous links to museums and other places of interest. The city of Stockholm operates the site <www.stockholm.se/english>, which has technical information about the city government, business information, and links to the Stockholm Information Service. General, useful information about Sweden and also about the cities of Stockholm, Göteborg, and Malmö can be found at <www.swedenguide.com>. Information about Uppsala can be found at <www.uppsala.se>.

WEIGHTS and MEASURES

For liquid and distance measures, see page 127. Sweden uses the metric system. You will find that Swedes use commas instead of full points to indicate decimals and use full points instead of commas to indicate thousands.

Length

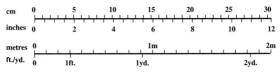

Weight

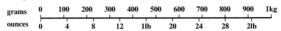

Temperature

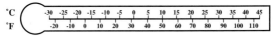

Fluid measures

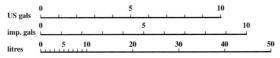

Distance

YOUTH HOSTELS (*vandrarhem*) (See also RECOMMENDED HOTELS, page 128.)

The Stockholm Information Service publishes an informative booklet *Hotels and Youth Hostels in Stockholm* that also lists hostels in the archipelago and around Lake Mälaren. Some are found in interesting places like boats and even an old prison, and you should expect to pay between 80–350kr per night, with breakfast and sheets extra.

Recommended Hotels

For further information on hotels, see page 105.

The price categories below are based on two people sharing a double room at full rates, including breakfast, Moms (Sales tax at 12%), and service charge. However, there are usually substantial discounts for weekends and during the summer season. Major credit cards are accepted everywhere.

$$$$	Above 2,000kr
$$$	1,250–2,000kr
$$	750–1,250kr
$	Below 750kr

STOCKHOLM

Modern Stockholm

Adlon Hotell $$$ *Vasagatan 42, SE-111 20; Tel. (08) 402 65 00; fax (08) 20 86 10; web site <www.adlon.se>.* Found close to Central Station in a building dating from 1884, this was established in 1944 and has always been privately-owned and -run independently of any chain. A designated IT hotel, your room can become your office. 78 rooms.

Berns Hotel $$$$ *Näckströmsgatan 8, SE-111 47; Tel. (08) 566 322 00; fax (08) 566 322 01; web site <www.berns.se>.* Small, intimate and exclusive hotel with rooms of varying sizes —one has its own sauna. All rooms have a distinguished contemporary décor designed around rich marble and cherry wood. 65 rooms.

Claes På Hörnet $$$ *Surbrunnsgatan 20, SE-113 48; Tel. (08) 16 51 30, fax (08) 612 53 15; e-mail <clas.pa.hornet@ telia.com>.* Once an 18th-century inn, it is now a small hotel with a charming ambiance. Situated in a quiet area north of the city center. 10 rooms.

First Hotel Reisen $$$$ *Skeppsbron 12, SE-111 30; Tel. (08) 22 32 60, fax (08) 20 15 59; web site <www.firsthotels. com>.* A nicely located and well-equipped 19th-century hotel on the Gamla Stan waterfront, overlooking Skeppsholmen. Sauna and piano bar. 144 rooms.

Grand Hôtel (5 star deluxe) $$$$ *S. Blaiseholmshamnen 8, P.O. Box 16424, SE-103 27; Tel. (08) 679 35 00; fax (08) 611 86 86; web site <www.grandhotel.se>.* Grand in size, architecture, style, and graciousness, it is the only hotel of its class in Sweden. Fantastic views across to the Royal Palace in Gamla Stan, and a Michelin star restaurant. 310 rooms.

Hotel Aldoria $$ *Sankt Eriksgatan 38, SE-112 34;Tel. (08) 693 63 00; fax (08) 693 63 33; web site <www.hotelaldoria. com>.* Found a little way outside the city center, this is a small, pleasant hotel with newly renovated rooms and suites. 23 rooms.

Hotell Anno 1647 (3 stars) $$$ *Mariagränd 3, SE-116 41; Tel. (08) 442 16 80; fax (08) 442 16 47; e-mail <info@ anno@swedenhotels.se>.* Dating from 1647, this hotel retains its old-world charm and is located in a historic setting at Slussen. Close to Gamla Stan and the ferry to Djurgården. 42 rooms.

Hotell August Strindberg $$ *Tegnergatan 38, Se-113 59; Tel. (08) 32 50 06; fax (08) 20 90 85; web site <www. hotellstrindberg.se>.* Named after the national author and artist whose statue is in the nearby park. Clean and comfortable rooms, all non-smoking. 21 rooms.

Hotel Birger Jarl (4 stars) $$$ *Tulegatan 8, Box 19016, SE-104 32; Tel. (08) 674 18 00; fax (08) 673 73 66; web site <www. birgerjarl.se>.* The only hotel in Stockholm with a Swedish designer profile, this has recently been enhanced by the addition of business rooms and 10 new specialty rooms on the 7th floor created by different designers. 230 rooms.

Hotell Diplomat $$$$ *Strandvägen 7C, Box 14059, SE-104 40; Tel. (08) 459 68 00; fax (08) 459 68 20; web site <www. diplomat-hotel.se>*. A delightful Jugend style building dating from 1911. Family owned, it has individually designed rooms and special business suites. Fine waterfront location, and just a short walk from city center. 128 rooms.

Hotel Esplanade $$$ *Strandvägen 7A, SE-114 56; Tel. (08) 663 07 40; fax (08) 662 59 92; web site <www.hotelesplanade. se>*. Behind a charming Jugend façade, this is a small, charming hotel with individually decorated rooms. Views over Nybroviken Bay, and just a short distance from the town center. 34 rooms.

Hotell Kung Carl (4 stars) $$$ *Birger Jarlsgatan 21, Box 1776, SE-111 87; Tel. (08) 463 50 00; fax (08) 463 50 50; web site <www.hkhotels.se>*. A historic hotel recently renovated and expanded to include new floors with exclusive business rooms. A fine, central location at Stureplan. 110 rooms.

Hotell Mälardrottningen $$ *Riddarholmen, SE-111 28; Tel. (08) 24 36 00, fax (08) 24 36 76; web site <www.malardrottningen. se>*. Stockholm's most unusual hotel. A 1920s luxury yacht formerly owned by American millionairess Barbara Hutton, now anchored at Riddarholmen — next to Gamla Stan. Cabins are now luxury hotel rooms. 58 rooms.

Hotel Sandström $$ *Sankt Eriksgatan 75, SE-113 32; Tel. (08) 30 83 32; fax (08) 30 74 46; web site <www. hotelsandstrom.nu>*. Away from the city center, this is found on the 5th floor and has rooms decorated in various historic fashions — try a 1930s or 1950s room. Breakfast included. 8 rooms.

Hotel Tre Små Rum $ *Högbergsgatan 81, SE-118 54; Tel. (08) 641 23 71; fax (08) 642 88 08; web site <www.tresmarum. se>.* A small bed and breakfast hotel located in Södermalm: To get there, take the Red Line, destination Norsborg, stop Mariatorget on the "T." 7 rooms.

Hotel Tegnérlunden (3 stars) $$$ *Tegnérlunden 8, SE-113 59; Tel. (08) 545 455 50; fax (08) 545 455 51; e-mail <info. tegner@swedenhotels.se>.* Located in a quiet square just off the pedestrian shopping street of Drottninggatan and a few minutes' walk from Central Station. Disabled and non-smoking rooms, rooftop breakfast room, and sauna. 103 rooms.

Hotel Terminus $$$ *Vasagatan 20, Box 271, SE-101 25; Tel. (08) 440 16 70; fax (08) 440 16 71; web site <www.terminus. se>.* A Best Western hotel in the center of town and directly across from Central Station. Comfortable, traditional ambiance. 155 rooms.

Långholmen Hotell $$ *Gamla Kronohäktet, Långholm-smuren 20, Box 9116, SE-102 72; Tel. (08) 668 05 00; fax (08) 720 85 75; web site <www.langholmen.com>.* On the island of Långholmen, this was built as a prison in the early 19th century, closed in 1972, then converted to an unusual hotel 14 years later. Expect captivatingly small rooms. 102 rooms.

Lydmar Hotel $$$$ *Sturegatan 10, SE-114 36; Tel. (08) 566 113 00; fax (08) 566 113 01; web site <www.lydmar.se>.* A block from Stureplan, this is a jazz lovers delight. Individually styled rooms, colorfully decorated with antiques, contemporary art and design, and photos of jazz and soul entertainers who have performed in the lobby restaurant. 62 rooms.

Radisson SAS Royal Viking Hotel $$$$ *Vasagatan 1, Box 234, SE-101 24; Tel. (08) 14 10 00, fax (08) 10 81 80; web site*

Stockholm

<www.radisson.com/stockholmse_royalviking>. An impressive building next to Central Station and airport buses. Bermuda Pool Club has pool, whirlpool, sauna, massage, and solarium. Fine fish restaurant and rooftop bar. 351 rooms.

Radisson SAS SkyCity Hotel $$$ *Sky City, SE-190 45 Stockholm-Arlanda; Tel. (08) 506 740 00; fax 506 740 01; web site <www.radisson.com/stockholmse_airport>*. Located in the Arlanda Airport and SkyCity complex. 230 rooms.

Radisson SAS Strand Hotel $$$$ *Nybrokajen 9, Box 16396, SE-103 27; Tel. (08) 678 78 00, fax (08) 611 24 36; web site <www.radisson.com/stockholmse_strand>*. Large, traditional, ivy-covered building overlooking the boats on Nybroviken Bay, best seen from the Meeting Point bar. 24-hour room service and sauna. 149 rooms.

Rica City Hotel Gamla Stan $$$ *Lilla Nygatan 25, SE-110 28; Tel. (08) 723 72 50, fax (08) 723 72 59; web site <www.rica.cityhotels.se>*. A converted 17th-century house at the Gamla Stan's south end. Quiet and tucked away, it was totally renovated in 1998 with all rooms decorated in an 18th-century Gustavian style. 51 rooms.

Rica City Hotel Kungsgatan $$$ *Kungsgatan 47, SE-111 56; Tel. (08) 723 72 72, fax (08) 723 72 79; web site <www.rica.cityhotels.se>*. A large city center hotel that has two floors of non-smoking rooms. Includes a Continental breakfast delivered to your door. 293 rooms.

Scandia Hotel Anglais $$$ *Humlegårdsgatan 23, SE-102 44; Tel. (08) 517 340 00, fax (08) 517 340 11; web site <www. scandic- hotels.com>*. A modern hotel, opposite Humlegården Park and just a short walk to Stureplan and the city center. 212 rooms.

Scandic Hotel Continental $$$$ *Vasagatan/Klar Vatugränd 4, SE-101 22; Tel. (08) 517 342 00, fax (08) 517 342 11; web site <www. scandic-hotels.com>*. Located in the city center across from Central Station. Voted "Best Business Hotel in Sweden 1999". 268 rooms.

Sergel Plaza Hotel (5 stars) $$$$ *Brunkebergstorg 9, Box 16411, SE-103 27; Tel. (08) 22 66 00; fax (08) 21 50 70; web site <www. provobis.se>*. Located in a quiet square in a central position just behind Sergels Torg and the Kulturhuset. A distinguished hotel with a charming lobby, piano bar, and a renowned restaurant. 75 rooms.

Sheraton Stockholm Hotel & Towers (5 stars) $$$$ *Tegelbacken 6, P.O. Box 195, SE-101 23; Tel. (08) 412 34 00; fax (08) 412 34 09*. Close to the Central Station and with fantastic views over Lake Mälaren, Gamla Stan, and City Hall. Unusually large excellently equipped modern rooms and suites. Special services on Tower Floor, casino, and sauna. 462 rooms.

Stockholm Plaza Hotel $$$ *Birger Jarlsgatan 29, Box 7707, SE-103 28; Tel. (08) 566 220 00, fax (08) 566 220 20; web site <www.elite.se/stockholmplaza>*. An unusual 19th-century façade fronts a hotel with a pleasing ambiance. Good location, very close to Stureplan. 151 rooms.

Gamla Stan (Old Town)

Lady Hamilton Hotel $$$$ *Storkyrkobrinken 5, SE-111 28; Tel. (08) 506 401 00; fax (08) 506 401 10; web site <www. lady-hamilton.se>*. This Class-A listed building dates from the late 15th century. Expect nautical memorabilia and antiques — including a collection of grandfather clocks. Take a dip in an early 14th-century well in the basement. 34 rooms.

Lord Nelson Hotel $$$ *Vasterlånggatan 22, SE-111 29; Tel. (08) 506 401 20, fax (08) 506 401 30; web site <www.lord- nelson.*

se>. A 17th-century Jugend-style house in Gamla Stan with a width of less than 5 m (16 ft), making it Sweden's narrowest hotel. A nautical flavor throughout fairly small rooms, basement sauna, and rooftop terrace. 31 rooms.

Victory Hotel $$$$ *Lilla Nygatan 5, SE-111 28; Tel. (08) 506 400 00; fax (08) 506 400 10; web site <www.victory-hotel.se>*. A 17th-century residence in Gamla Stan now a small, intimate *Relais & Chateaux* hotel, named after Lord Nelson's flagship. Rooms individually decorated with antiques — some with IT options. Bar, sauna, and an excellent restaurant. 45 rooms.

UPPSALA

Radisson SAS Hotel Gillet $$$$ *Dragarbrunnsgatan 23, P.O. Box 1234, SE-751 42; Tel. (018) 15 53 60, fax (018) 15 33 80; web site <www.radisson.com/uppsalase>*. An excellent location in the center of town. Pool, sauna, solarium, and excellent restaurant. 160 rooms.

YOUTH HOSTELS

Af Chapman & Skeppsholmen *Flaggmansvägen 8, Skeppsholmen, SE-111 49 Skeppshol-men; Tel. (08) 463 22 66; fax (08) 611 71 55; web site <www.merasverige.nu>*. Located in a landmark 1888 ship, this hostel has a spectacular view of Gamla Stan. Advance reservations recommended during summer. Open all year. 290 beds.

Långholmens Vandrarhem *Gamla Kronohäktet, Långholmsmuren 20, Box 9116, SE-102 72; Tel. (08) 668 05 10; fax (08) 720 85 75; web site <www.langholmen.com>*. This is an excellent hostel on the island of Längholmen, located within an old prison building. 26 beds open all year and 254 beds in summer and on weekends.

Recommended Restaurants

Stockholm offers a variety of restaurants. Portions are usually generous and salad is often included. On a tight budget, however, make lunch (*dagens rätt*) the main meal, and look for offers such as Sunday specials. Tourist information publications such as *What's On* give listings. Remember that some restaurants may be closed during July.

Eating out in Sweden can be expensive; one reason is that the bill usually includes 21% Moms (VAT) and a service charge. It is customary to round up the bill to the nearest 10kr.

The establishments listed below offer both quality food and service, and represent good value for money. Prices are for an evening meal for two without wine. All establishments take major credit cards.

$$$$	over 1,000kr
$$$	500–1,000kr
$$	300–500kr
$	150–300kr

STOCKHOLM

Modern Stockholm

Berns $$/$$$ *Berzelii Park; Tel. (08) 566 322 22; web site <www.berns.se>*. Opened in 1863 — with an opulent 19th-century interior open-air veranda, this was a renowned restaurant and cabaret spot for over 100 years. Redesigned by Terence Conran, it is now a delightful restaurant and bar complex. The main restaurant (closed in July and open for dinner Monday–Saturday), offers the best of modern European cuisine. The Bar & Grill specializes in grills and spit roasts, and opens daily for lunch and dinner.

Bon Lloc $$$/$$$$ *Bergsgatan 33; Tel. (08) 650 50 82*. Monday–Friday lunch and dinner, Saturday dinner. Mathias

Stockholm

Dahlgren has earned a Michelin star for this restaurant that excels in preparing Modern Mediterranean cuisine.

Clas På Hörnet $$/$$$ *Surbrunnsgatan 20; Tel. (08) 16 51 36; web site <www.kvartersmenyn.com>.* Monday–Friday lunch and dinner, Saturday dinner. Found in the delightful 18th-century building of the same name, this is the place for traditional Swedish cuisine in a charming ambiance.

Die Ecke $$ Tegelbacken 6; Tel. (08) 412 34 72. Open daily for lunch and dinner. A genuine German restaurant in décor and cuisine, located in a corner of the Sheraton Hotel. Schnitzels, sausages, and strudels, washed down, of course, with real German beer.

Edsbacka Krog $$$$ *Sollentunavägen 222, Solna; Tel. (08) 850 815.* Located in the grounds of a 19th-century palace, a short distance from the city center. With two Michelin stars, it's known as Stockholm's most expensive restaurant and one of the first licensed inns in the country. The food and service is worth the price. Excellent *smorgäsbord* lunch served.

Eriks Bakficka $$$ *Fredrikshovsgatan 4; Tel. (08) 660 15 99.* Monday–Friday lunch and dinner, Saturday and Sunday dinner. Found just off of Strandvägen near the Djurgårdsbron bridge, this is run by Erik Lallerstedt of Gondolen fame. The "Back Pocket" is more relaxed but no less refined, with super Swedish dishes and celebrity clientele.

Franska Matsalen $$$/$$$$ *Grand Hotel, S Blasieholmen 8; Tel. (08) 679 35 00, web site <www.grandhotel.se>.* Monday–Friday, dinner. Particularly elegant, with mahogany panelling and crystal chandeliers, and elected Sweden's Best Restaurant by *Gourmet Magazine*. Swedish cuisine prepared with a French touch, a fine selection of French cheese, and a very good wine cellar with over 25,000 bottles. Magnificent views over Gamla Stan and Stockholm's waterways.

Fredsgatan 12 $$$ *Fredsgatan 12; Tel. (08) 24 80 52.* Lunch Monday–Friday and dinner Saturday. Across the street from the Swedish Cabinet offices and on the ground floor of the Academy of Art, this attracts a government crowd at lunchtime, and locals and visitors for dinner. Expect a modern dining room with an innovative menu in the Swedish and international style, plus an interesting drink menu. One Michelin star.

Gondolen $$$ *Stadsgården 6; Tel. (08) 641 70 90.* Monday–Saturday, lunch and dinner. Located in Slussen at the top of the Katarina Elevator this fine restaurant is a tourist attraction in its own right. Really, the cuisine and views match each other with their excellence.

Kungshallen $ *Kungsgatan 44; Tel. (08) 21 80 05; web site <www.kungshallen.com>.* Near Hötorget, this is said to be Scandinavia's largest restaurant hall. With fourteen restaurants catering to very different tastes, there's bound to be something here for everyone.

Liberty Kitchen $$/$$$ *Tegelbacken 6; Tel. (08) 412 34 72.* Daily lunch and dinner. Unusually located in the lobby of the Sheraton Hotel with an open-plan kitchen. A creative menu: varied appetizers, pizzas, specialties, steaks, pastas, and tempting desserts.

Opera Bar $$$ *Operahuset; Tel. (08) 676 58 01.* Meeting place for Stockholm's artistic elite ever since it opened in 1904. Splendid art deco interior with comfortable leather armchairs and marble-topped tables. Enjoy a drink and home-cooked Swedish dishes.

Stockholm

Operakällaren $$$/$$$$ *Operahuset; Tel. (08) 676 58 01, web site <www.operakallaren.com>.* Open daily for dinner, closed July. A venerable institution, dating back some 200 years, with a dining room considered the most beautiful in Sweden. Serving haute cuisine and especially famous for its wonderful smörgåsbord, it has a magnificent wine cellar considered the best-stocked in the country.

PA & CO $$/$$$ *Riddargatan 8; Tel. (08) 611 08 45.* Monday–Sunday dinner. Unpretentious in style and location, this restaurant, run by two pairs of brothers, has earned a reputation for innovation that attracts many guests of local importance to savor its delicacies. No reservations taken, so get there early.

Paul & Norbert $$$$ *Strandvägen 9; Tel. (08) 663 81 83.* Open Monday–Saturday for dinner. A small, luxury bistro with a minimalist, modern dining room. French nouvelle cuisine with a modern touch, the delightful eight-course gourmet menu is more than tempting, even at 1,050/1,300kr per person. À la carte dishes are charged by the plate, and become proportionally cheaper as you order more.

Stadshuskällaren $$$/$$$$ *Stadshuset; Tel. 650 54 54.* Monday–Friday dinner, Saturday lunch and dinner (reservation required). Found in the basement of City Hall, come here to savor a Nobel Banquet. In fact, your dinner will consist of the menu and wines served to the Nobel Prize winners the previous 10 December.

Strindbergs $$ *Drottninggatan 85; Tel. (08) 20 16 50.* Open daily for lunch and dinner. Located in an old grocery store on the ground floor of a building where August Strindberg lived. Original shelves line the walls of the bar, and an interesting selection of traditional dishes is on the small menu.

T/bar $$/$$$ *Strandvägen 7C; Tel. (08) 459 68 02; web site* <*www.hoteldiplomat.com*>. Open daily for lunch and dinner. A modern, pleasing restaurant located on the ground floor of the Hotel Diplomat with views over the water. Interesting mixed menu ranging from club sandwiches to poached *smögen* cod with scampi.

Wedholms Fisk $$$/$$$$ (many daily prices) *Nybrokajan 17; Tel. (08) 611 78 74.* Monday–Friday lunch and dinner, Saturday dinner. Considered by many to be Stockholm's premier seafood restaurant, and holder of a Michelin star. A plain but distinguished dining room. No ingredients or presentation can compete with the fish — the freshest and most varied selection in town.

GAMLA STAN (OLD TOWN)

Bistro Ruby $$$ *Österlänggatan 14; Tel. (08) 20 57 76.* Open daily for lunch and dinner. A lovely, small and intimate old-style Swedish dining room that makes a romantic ambiance. It serves Swedish dishes with a French flavor.

Den Gyldene Freden $$$/$$$$ *Österlånggatan 51; Tel. (08) 10 90 46.* Dinner Monday–Friday, lunch and dinner Saturday, closed July. Stockholm's most prestigious restaurant, it opened in 1772 and was named the "Golden Peace" after the peace treaty with Russia in 1721. The Swedish cuisine, superb service, and original atmosphere are not to be missed.

Eriks $$ *Österlånggatan 17; Tel. (08) 23 85 00.* Erik Lallerstedt, one of Sweden's finest chefs, presides over this restaurant in medieval Gamla Stan. The many tantalizing fish specialities include salmon dishes and grilled crayfish with a garlic-and-parsley flavored chablis sauce.

Gamla Stans Bryggeri $$ *Skeppsbrokajen Tullhus 2; Tel. (08) 20 20 65.* Open daily for lunch and dinner; open until 3am on weekends. Found on the quayside next to luxury yachts. A very large, partly open-air brewery (*bryggeri*) restaurant with good food and tasty fresh (*färsköl*) beer.

Järnet Matsal & Bar $$ *Österlänggatan 34-36; Tel. (08) 10 71 37; web site <www.jarnet.nu>.* Monday–Saturday, lunch and dinner. Select from a small but varied menu in this unpretentious, charming restaurant. In the popular bar, ask for their throat burning specialty — vodka with honey and hot peppers marinated in the bottle.

Leijontornet $$$ *Lilla Nygatan 5; Tel. (08) 14 23 55; web site <www.leijontornet.se>.* Dinner Monday–Saturday, closed July. High-class and traditional Swedish cuisine in a historic setting, with a glass door over the ruins of medieval walls. Located within the Victory Hotel.

Mälardrottningen $$/$$$ *Riddarholmen; Tel. (08) 24 36 00; web site <www.malardrottningen.se>.* International and Swedish cuisine is served on the Mälardrottningen, once Barbara Hutton's luxury yacht, which is now docked on the Riddarholmen quayside. Fine, varied dishes. On a fine evening, dining on the open deck offers one of the finest views of Stockhom.

Mårten Trotzig $$$ *Västerlånggatan 79; Tel. (08) 24 02 31.* Monday–Friday lunch and dinner, dinner only Saturday and Sunday. A new and instantly successful contemporary restaurant named after a 16th-century German businessman and set around the courtyard of an ancient building. Dining room on different levels, including one in the kitchen itself. Small menu of first-rate fish and meat dishes.

Pontus in the Green House $$$$ *Österlånggatan 17; Tel. (08) 23 85 00; web site <www.pontusigamlastan.se>.* Monday–Saturday, lunch and dinner. One of the finest restaurants in Stockholm. For a real culinary treat, sample chef Pontus Frithiof's multicourse, beautifully balanced and very creative dinners — approximately 965kr per person. Less from the à la carte menu or when you eat at the bar.

Siam $ *Stora Nygatan 25; Tel. (08) 20 02 33.* Open daily for lunch and dinner. The only Thai restaurant in Gamla Stan and located, incongruously, in 17th-century cellars. Lunch specials from 60kr and three course dinners start at 99kr.

Stortorgskällaren $$$ *Stortorget 7; Tel. (08) 10 55 33; web <www.stortorget.org>.* Open daily for lunch and dinner. In either brick-lined cellars or a large covered terrace overlooking the ancient square, you can taste traditional Swedish cuisine that changes seasonally.

Zum Franziskaner $$ *Skeppsbron 44; Tel. (08) 411 83 30.* Monday–Saturday, lunch and dinner. Stockholm's oldest restaurant; founded in the early 15th century, this is the third building on the site since 1600! With a traditional Jugendstil ambiance, its menu changes twice a year but always includes Swedish and German specialties.

UPPSALA

Domtrappkällaren $ *Sankt Eriksgränd 15; Tel. (018) 130955.* French and Swedish cuisines served in a cellar dating from the 14th century. Located near the cathedral. Specialities include delicious salmon and reindeer, as well as other fresh game dishes. Reservations necessary.

INDEX